HEALING
ALCOHOLISM

OTHER BOOKS BY CLAUDE M. STEINER

PUBLISHED BY GROVE PRESS

Readings in Radical Psychiatry (Claude M. Steiner, ed.)
Scripts People Live

HEALING ALCOHOLISM

Claude M. Steiner

Grove Press, Inc./New York

First Edition 1979
First Printing 1979
ISBN: 0-394-50860-2
Grove Press ISBN: 0-8021-0189-5
Library of Congress Catalog Card Number: 79-2320

Library of Congress Cataloging in Publication Data

Steiner, Claude, 1935–
    Healing alcoholism.

    Bibliography: p.
    Includes index.
    1. Alcoholism—Treatment.   2. Alcoholism—Psy-
chological aspects.   3. Alcoholics—Rehabilitation.
I. Title.
HV5050.S73   616.8′61′06   79-2320
ISBN 0-394-50860-2

Manufactured in the United States of America

Distributed by Random House, Inc., New York

GROVE PRESS, INC., 196 West Houston Street, New York, N.Y. 10014

To Denali

Contents

Acknowledgments

Everyone who ten years ago received my appreciation in *Games Alcoholics Play* deserves renewed thanks, for this book is built upon what I wrote then. Accordingly, I wish to again acknowledge the contributions made, many years ago, by Patricia Crossman, George David, John Dusay, Martin Groder, Stephen Karpman, Jack Leibman, Neil Ross, and Robert Zechnick. Most especially I want to thank Eric Berne for teaching me transactional analysis and psychiatry, and David Geisinger and Melissa Farley for their continuing friendship, feedback, and support all these years.

This is, however, a completely new work and since it is based on a great deal of practical experience I wish to thank, first and foremost, the many people who have trusted me in the last sixteen years to help them with their troubles, especially those who allowed me to see them through to their victories. From them I gleaned the data which justify the points of view expressed in this book.

Thanks are due to Hogie Wyckoff, who, during our love and work partnership, taught me the refinements of nurturing, new to this book, and who was a full participant with me in the development of the theory of radical psychiatry.

Thanks are also due to Darca Nicholson for teaching me about roundness and helping me to see that everything is connected to everything else. More specifically, she showed me that we are what we eat, and demonstrated to me the reality of healing.

To the members of the Bay Area Radical Psychiatry Collective—Becky Jenkins, Beth Roy, Bruce Dodson, Jude La Barre,

Robert Schwebel, Hogie Wyckoff, Darca Nicholson, and Michael Singer—thanks for the ongoing constructive criticism which has kept my perceptions sharp, my arguments cogent, and my heart open.

Thanks to the many observers-in-training who attended my groups and training meetings over the years, and who contributed their perceptions, their physical presence, and their therapeutic selves, expecting nothing in return but the chance to learn healing skills: Mary Selkirk, George Stokes, Libby Edwards, Bruce Dodson, Jude La Barre, Becky Jenkins, and Shelby Morgan.

I am grateful to Alan Rinzler, my editor, for the several critical readings and feedback which brought this book to its final form. I am thankful also to Leora Adler, a member of the Round Mountain Cooperative Community in Ukiah, California, who, between building yurts, attending meetings, and working in the vegetable garden, found time to type the final manuscript. Finally, I want to acknowledge Round Mountain, in whose peaceful shade stands the Cooperative Healing Center, where I wrote this book.

Preface

When I wrote *Games Alcoholics Play* [1] in 1968, I was an up-and-coming psychologist writing his first book, advocating a daring new point of view in the field of alcoholism: "An alcoholic can, under special circumstances return to social drinking." At that time, I did not drink at all, and I derived all my knowledge about alcohol and other drugs from my work with alcoholics at the Center for Special Problems, a public clinic for alcoholics in San Francisco, the therapeutic mecca of North American alcoholism. In my book, I addressed fellow professionals and spoke over the heads of the actual victims of alcoholism: the addicts themselves and their relatives, friends, and coworkers.

Today, ten years later, the daring idea of the sixties has become commonplace knowledge. The data confirming the possibility that some unquestioned alcoholics return to normal or social drinking continues to mount. Finally, in 1978, a research project sponsored by the Rand Corporation, and undertaken by Armor, Polich, and Stambul, [2] concluded: "There seems no choice but to entertain the possibility that some alcoholics return to a pattern of drinking without necessarily exhibiting alcoholic symptoms." Thus someone who has been an alcoholic is not necessarily always an alcoholic.

Games Alcoholics Play has been a well-read, much-appreciated, as well as much-maligned book. But as I reread it over the years, I found that I became increasingly dissatisfied with it.

Most rankling was the tone of the book. Even considering that I spoke as a dissident and took disrespectful jabs at alcoologists' pomp, my own pronouncements had a fatuous sound of their own.

My point about the alcoholic's possible return to social drinking was not adequately explained and has been misunderstood. In some A.A. (Alcoholics Anonymous) circles, I have been accorded the status of a public enemy second only to alcohol itself.

On the other hand, I have found that people who agreed with me were taking my statements about avoiding Rescues as permission to behave in a heartless and callous way in their work with alcoholics. When this attitude permeated agencywide policies, it became more than a little distressing to me.

Finally, I have learned a great deal more about alcoholism since I wrote *Games Alcoholics Play*. This book, therefore, is a mixture of a few tried-and-tested ideas which appeared in my first book and a lot of new ideas which I have had and used effectively since, plus some clarifications and some corrections. Now I am a more seasoned psychotherapist who has worked with and followed numbers of clients through successful experiences in making their lives work. Among them were alcoholics who have confirmed many of my earlier notions—especially that alcoholism can be healed, completely and permanently.

In *Games Alcoholics Play*, I wrote for my fellow professionals and hoped to make sense to alcoholics; in this new book, I am writing for the alcoholic (and his or her social circle) hoping to make sense to my fellow professionals. My emphasis in the first book was Transactional Analysis, script analysis, and the theory of alcoholism in general. In this book I will spend less space theorizing and will write mostly about the practical aspects of—and solutions to—that great debilitating plague, alcoholism. (For a more complete text on scripts and script analysis, see *Scripts People Live*.[3])

My own life over the past ten years reflects the changes which this book has undergone. I am less brash and cocksure, and hopefully wiser. I no longer call the people I work for "my patients" nor do I call myself or invite them to call me "Dr. Steiner." I have smoked marijuana, taken my share of LSD and other hallucinogens and drink a very moderate amount, every so often: mostly beer and an occasional margarita when dining out. On the other hand, I have stopped smoking cigarettes and have drastically cut down my consumption of coffee, sugar, beef and other red meats. I enjoy getting high and have noticed the subtle differences in quality and duration of the intoxicating effects of different drugs.

Once a staunch defender of marijuana as a safe drug, I have come to realize that it, too, has its problem; more subtle and not as damaging as alcohol, but nonetheless real.

I have gained new knowledge about why some people use drugs and some don't. I have come to realize that alcohol is just one substance of many which people use and misuse.

I am lucky in that I have never been able to ignore the side effects of drugs. Cigarettes made me nauseous; I was not able to smoke more than about five a day. Alcohol gives me headaches, coffee "wires" me up, aspirin upsets my stomach, antibiotics dull my brain, narcotics let me down hard, marijuana interferes with my thinking and stays in my system, sugar burns my tongue, food coloring tastes bitter, nitrates and nitrites give me diarrhea, and meat feels heavy in my gut. I seem to have a ready-made anti-substance-abuse mechanism. I believe that everyone is capable of sensitivity to the harmful side effects of substances we ingest, and that developing this sensitivity is the most effective way of struggling against all forms of drug abuse.

Since the beginning of recorded history, people have used easily accessible substances such as wine, marijuana, opium, mescaline, psilocybin, coffee, tea, coca leaves, and tobacco, to "get high"—to make themselves feel good, or at least better.

Lately (in the last few centuries) we have added to these substances refined chemicals that get us high: 90-proof liquor, morphine, cocaine, THC, LSD, amphetamines, and barbiturates. Further, we have used chemicals to "improve" our food, and many of these (such as saccharin, food dyes, and nitrites) are slowly being found to be harmful. Others, like refined sugar, are intoxicating as well. At this point, whether we want it or not, we are a nation of people addicted to refined chemicals and adulterated foods.

I believe that the increasing consumption of refined chemicals and foods plays a very important part in alcoholism and other drug abuse because these additives completely dull and destroy our innate sensitivities to the harmful side effects of what we put in our mouths. If alcohol is hard to fight by itself, it is far harder to deal with in combination with processed foods, sugar, coffee, food additives, and cigarettes (with all that is added to *them*). The destructive aftereffects of all the things we ingest become more and more complicated and hidden (like radioactivity, for which we have no sensors), until their aftereffects manifest themselves, usually too late to do anything about them.

Alcoholics are just a subgroup of the population who, along with other addicts—like tobacco, sugar, coffee, and heroin addicts as well as aspirin, laxative and bicarb addicts—represent a logical extension of everybody else's drug abuse.

This is all to say, in a roundabout way, that alcoholism is everybody's problem—not only the problem of twenty million hard-core drunks. We are either alcoholics ourselves or our loved ones are, or we sell or profit from alcohol, or we tolerate its sale and promotion, or we use other drugs the way alcoholics use alcohol. One way or another, most of us play the addiction game. When you are talking about, looking at, providing for, or punishing an alcoholic, you could easily be talking about, looking at, providing for, or punishing yourself. We are all in this together; none of us is safe. So, if you are ready to read about yourself (and me) and how we can work together to heal our alcoholic life-styles head on, I believe that you will find this book to be a useful new look into the problem.

Introduction

Since becoming an "alcohologist" (that's what we experts in alcoholism are called—I am not sure I'm flattered) I have noticed that alcoholism affects an amazing number of people. Every so often I randomly ask people I meet whether their lives have been touched by alcoholism. The proportion of those who answer yes is truly amazing: between 80 and 90 percent. "My father, (mother, uncle, sister, brother) is (was) an alcoholic" is the most frequent reply. Neighbors, business partners, and coworkers are often mentioned. Occasionally someone will report having been victimized by alcoholics, as in the case of the woman whose husband was killed in a head-on collision with an alcoholic driving the wrong way on a one-way street.

By the time a person has reached middle age, it is almost inevitable that he or she will have had at least one serious brush with alcoholism. Many will have to deal with it oftener and earlier in their lives, some will be born into it. It seems that we all have had that sudden recognition that someone we knew was crossing that nebulous line between a little too much drinking and alcoholism. We have all watched with horror the dilapidating condition of a relative or coworker after regular nightly drinking bouts, or felt the acceptance of before, during, and after-dinner drinking attempting to pass as good cheer. We have heard of or witnessed the dreadful binges ending in hospitalization and experienced the sinking feeling of seeing a recovered alcoholic begin the slow but steady descent into alcoholic hell as he protested the absolute harmlessness of his drinking. Or we may ourselves suddenly have had the shocking realization that our once-easygoing drinking has become tough going, and that we have lost control over alcohol and feel powerless to do anything about it.

Alcoholism continues to rise; in a recent Gallup poll conducted in 1978 by the C. F. Kettering Foundation, 23 percent of Americans polled admitted occasional overindulgence in alcohol in 1978 as against 18 percent in 1977, an increase of 5 percent in one year. In 1978, 25 percent said that alcohol-related problems have adversely affected their family lives, against 12 percent in 1974; an increase of 13 percent in four years (San Francisco *Chronicle*, July 3, 1978). That is a doubling from about 25 million to 50 million in four years, or 8 million new people adversely affected every year.

Alcoholism is pervasive; but when we look at it from a certain perspective, we notice that alcoholism is just one component of a pattern of addiction to chemicals. Alcoholism is just the most notorious such addiction; a case of 20 million people's impotence in the face of a single powerful substance.

The power of alcohol is awesome not only in numbers of people affected but also in the grip it has on individuals. It isn't unusual for an alcoholic who has been sober for ten or more years to return to his previous alcoholic state, as if no healing or improvement had occurred. For Alcoholics Anonymous this is taken as evidence that alcoholism is incurable; it is a disease which may go into remission, but which continues to develop and is inevitably activated by a single drink.

One of A.A.'s official publications states:

> We alcoholics are men and women who have lost the ability to control our drinking. We know that no real alcoholic *ever* regains control. All of us felt at times that we were regaining control ... [but] we are convinced to a man that alcoholics of our type are in the grip of a progressive illness. Over any period of time we get worse, never better. ... Physicians who are familiar with alcoholism agree that there is no such thing as making a normal drinker out of an alcoholic.[1]

The views of A.A. are highly respected in the professional community, as well they might be; when the criterion is sobriety,

A.A. has achieved more success than any other approach. The American Medical Association publishes a *Manual on Alcoholism* [2] in which A.A.'s views are echoed. According to this manual, alcoholism is a "... highly complex illness ... characterized by preoccupation with alcohol and loss of control over its consumption such as to lead to intoxication when drinking is begun; by chronicity; by progression and by tendency towards relapse."

In the sophisticated language of the medical brotherhood, the above statement claims that alcoholism is not only an illness, but an incurable one. However, the problem with this claim is that the term "illness" has a very specific meaning. Using the medical definition, an illness is " ... an interruption or perversion of function of any of the organs, or an acquired morbid change in any tissue of an organism or throughout an organism, with characteristic symptoms caused by specific micro-organismal alterations."[3]

There is no evidence that alcoholism satisfies the definition of an illness. Take the example of a thirty-year alcoholic who has been sober for three years. He is in good health and there are no signs or traces in his bodily tissue of any interruption or perversion of any of the organs, any morbid change or any micro-organismal alterations. Yet tomorrow he may go down to the corner bar, have a drink, and within a week be on the skids again. We have plenty of evidence that this is possible.

Where is the evidence that alcoholism is an illness? I have seen none. All of the years of scientific search for evidence of it have failed to produce convincing—let alone conclusive—proof.

It is A.A. dogma that alcoholism is a disease; some members insist that it is an allergy. To support their contention, they cite the fact that some people react violently to alcohol from the very first. The reaction seems to be to the alcohol as a chemical in the same manner in which allergic people react to penicillin, poison oak, or pollen. It is true that some alcoholics swear that they react to alcohol with a violence similar to that of acute allergies and that they remember acting in that manner from the very first time they touched alcohol; one sip of the stuff, and complete drunkenness followed. But the similarity seems overdrawn. First: only a very small minority of people have that kind of reaction. Secondly: the reaction is like no other allergy. Allergies result in a systemic reaction to a minute quantity of the allergen. The incapacity to stop drinking even one drink could be called a systemic reaction to alcohol (which is not quite a minute quantity), I suppose; but if alcoholism is an allergy, it stands alone among all the others—invented especially, it seems, to satisfy A.A.'s need to prove that it is a physical illness. In any case, I am sure that A.A. would frown upon any medical experiments to find a drug that could cure alcoholics of their allergy.

Instead, it seems that some people are constitutionally sensitive to alcohol. For example, the one and only time that I was ever really drunk was the very first time I drank alcohol. I was about fourteen years old. My parents threw a party, and I helped wash glasses. A few of the glasses still had a little rum and Coca-Cola left in them, and I drank them for the taste of the Coke. Suddenly, to my surprise, I was completely smashed. Allergy? I don't think so. I never drank in excess again and was never compelled to. This is just one example; another example is the seeming vulnerability of Native Americans to alcohol and eventual alcoholism.

It's a well-known fact that Native Americans as a group seem defenseless against the ravages of alcohol. Some say that proves the allergy theory. To me it shows only that the sensitively tuned body reacts strongly to alcohol and that Native Americans found it and still find it a solution to their intolerable sorrows. I am willing to consider that there are inherited differences in people's reaction to alcohol and that some Native Americans have a genetic sensitivity to alcohol just as red-haired Caucasians have a genetic sensitivity to the sun. People are different from each other, their reaction to drugs are different from each other, and these differences have a genetic component. That much is obvious. But who becomes alcoholic and how it happens is not only genetic or purely physical—or for that matter especially just psychological.

To say that alcoholism is an illness is to say that it has an exclusively physical basis. In this sense, as Thomas Szasz points out,[4] the word "illness" is used as a metaphor; such as when the president of the United States says our economy is ill, or when Martin Luther King said that racism is a disease that infects all of us. The word "illness" is used in an imprecise sense.

It may be beneficial for an alcoholic to learn that he is not a common drunk, but is ill. I am sure that a person who makes herself a public nuisance while drunk would prefer to be taken to a nice hospital to have her illness treated than to be thrown in the drunk tank as a common criminal. In fact, the concept of alcoholism as an illness was introduced partially in the same humanitarian spirit in which the concept of mental illness was invented—as an effort to clean up the public image of the mad and inebriated, and in order to convince the authorities that the treatment they were getting as common criminals (or worse) was inhumane and counterproductive. This was a definite service to those who were plagued by these afflictions. Being considered ill feels better than being considered a no-good bum. Hospitals are usually better places than prisons. But it is not accurate to call the mad and inebriated ill, for the most part, and therefore only partially helpful because it is only, at best, half-true.

However, not all the motivation for the "medicalization" of alcoholism and emotional disturbance is benign in intent. Another motive is what has been called "medical imperialism"; the tendency of the medical industry, strongly backed by pharmaceutical interests, to include more and more aspects of human affliction under its control. Under the influence of this tendency, everything that goes wrong with people—alcoholism, drug abuse, sexual problems, and unhappiness of all sorts—should be looked after by a physician (who will surely collect his fees) and treated with drugs (which will cost plenty). This makes doctors, drug companies, and druggists happy, but it is not so good for the recipients of the treatment. To compound the problem, some of the difficulties which have been taken over by the medical establishment (alcoholism, schizophrenia, depression) have been declared incurable because no one (especially not physicians) seems to know what to do about them except to drug their victims into some form of relief.

As an example, alcoholism is defined as a chronic, progressive illness. Accordingly, the *Manual on Alcoholism* recommends that it be treated "in much the same way as are other chronic and relapsing medical conditions (in which) the aim of treatment is then viewed more as one of control than cure." [5] In plain English: "Alcoholism is incurable. The best that can be done is to control it and make the patient comfortable."

Any professional that goes along with this understanding of

alcoholism will be badly prepared for dealing with a person who has a drinking problem. What could be more depressing for a physician than to treat someone with the mere purpose of control rather than cure? Actually, most doctors shudder at the idea of adding an alcoholic to their clientele. Alcoholics are undisciplined, they don't pay their bills, they call at all hours of the day and night, and are insulting and insensitive to the physician's feelings and needs when they are drunk. They don't listen, they don't follow doctor's orders, and they are extremely depressing patients. Physicians are people, and like any other working people, they like to be effective in their work. Alcoholism is an area where they have little to offer and where failure and depression for both patient and doctor is the expectation. Medical imperialism is oppressive to physicians as well, and profits only those doctors who care strictly about money. Some enlightened physicians are beginning to realize how their profession's grab for power works to their own disadvantage. They increasingly support having people other than physicians share in the health care of the population. They are willingly decreasing their own power and incomes, but they do it knowing that everyone's health—including their own—is improved in the process.

But the confusion about alcoholism is even more serious than that. The opposition to the view that alcoholism can be cured is massive and comes primarily from A.A. and A.A.-oriented physicians. Denying that there are cures tends to cut off interest in those therapeutic approaches that might work. In addition, there is evidence that when the therapist expects a patient to fail in therapy, failure does occur. Frank [6] has demonstrated that expectancy and hope in the therapist, when transmitted to the client, is a powerful factor which determines the outcome of the therapy. Hope in the healer and in the patient is a powerful factor in healing.

I believe that alcoholics are neither incurable nor ill (unless they are in the midst of withdrawal or have liver disease or some other alcohol-related illness), and I say so to the people I work for. This belief is the first in a series of reasons which make me an effective therapist for alcoholics. In addition to expecting success, I have learned with the help of my clients, colleagues, and friends, what to do to help the alcoholic stop being an alcoholic. This book presents views and approaches to the problem which I have developed over the years. Although the book often speaks of therapy, and might be thought irrelevant to people who are not therapists, I believe that all readers can profit from these insights, which can be applied by therapists and nontherapists alike.

PART ONE

What Is Alcoholism?

1

The Alcoholic Game

Why People Drink

If alcoholism is not a disease, then what is it? I believe that the simplest and yet most valid definition of alcoholism is that it is a *very bad habit*. The habit of alcoholism can be acquired in a number of different ways. Not all alcoholics are the same, and they become alcoholic in different ways and for different reasons. There seem to be three major reasons for alcoholism. One is physical or physiological, based on the fact that alcohol is a very powerful, mind- and body-altering drug, effective in reducing anxiety and bringing about well-being (getting people high), but also addictive. By addictive, I mean: (a) that, as you drink more and more, you will need more and more alcohol to get the same effect; and (b) that when you get addicted, you will get physically sick (withdrawal sickness) for a while if you stop drinking for any length of time.

The second reason is social. People become alcoholics because drinking is taught and promoted by our parents, relatives, and coworkers. It is always present when people are having fun and relaxing. It is often required as part of the public-relations aspect of being employed. It is heavily pushed by the advertising media. It is generally encouraged and tolerated by the whole society.

Third: people acquire the bad habit of alcoholism for psychological reasons; because very often drinking is the simplest, most effective solution available for coping with personal problems. For example, people are often confronted with a life situation for which they have literally no visible solution. We do not enjoy the state of powerlessness we experience when we cannot solve our problems. For some, drinking blots out perceptions of powerlessness and anxiety. It gives a sense of well-being, detachment, and power which is, in effect, the best possible solution for the situation at hand.

There are a few other reasons why people drink. When properly prepared, alcohol is a delight to the palate. Alcohol also has some definite, beneficial medical effects. People who drink for taste or medicine sometimes get addicted to alcohol.

Alcoholism as a Game

In addition to *why* people drink we can also describe *how* they drink. People's drinking patterns vary; they play the game in different ways.

People have played games for a long time, but Eric Berne was the first to analyze and diagram the games that people play. In his astonishing best-seller, *Games People Play*,[1] he described a number of games. Included among them, under the heading of "Life Games," was the game of "Alcoholism."

A game is a repetitive transaction, with a beginning, middle, and end, which has a covert motive, or payoff. Alcoholism, as a game is a repetitive pattern (as we all know) which has identifiable beginning, middle, and end stages, and which is played by the alcoholic for reasons that are not entirely obvious to the observer.

A game is a set of transactions between people. The different people who play the game will take roles in the game. According to Berne, the roles of Alcoholism are: It (the Alcoholic), the Rescuer, the Persecutor, the Patsy, and the Connection. Berne pointed out that people who play one role in the game will usually take another role sooner or later. It is important to remember that a game is a social event which involves more than one person and that it is not possible for a person to play a game alone. Accordingly, the alcoholic could not play his game by himself; he needs to recruit into his life people who are willing to interact with him so that the game can go through its several stages (the beginning, middle, and end). Without others to play the roles in the game, the alcoholic could get only to the first transaction and would have to stop. This important concept—that it takes two to play a game—is one of the contributions of Transactional Analysis game theory to the understanding of human behavior.

This is Eric Berne's description, of the game of Alcoholic in *Games People Play,* (slightly abridged):

In game analysis there is no such thing as alcoholism or "an alcoholic," but there is a role called the Alcoholic in a certain type of game. If a biochemical or physiological abnormality is the prime mover in excessive drinking—and that is still open to some question—then its study belongs in the field of internal medicine. Game analysis is interested in something quite different—the kinds of social transactions that are related to such excesses. Hence the game "Alcoholic."

In its full flower this is a five-handed game, although the roles may be condensed so that it starts off and terminates as a two-handed one. The central role is that of the Alcoholic—the one who·is "it"—played by White. The chief supporting role is that of Persecutor, typically played by a member of the opposite sex, usually the spouse. The third role is that of Rescuer, usually played by someone of the same sex, often the good family doctor who is interested in the patient and also in drinking problems. In the classical situation the doctor successfully rescues the alcoholic from his habit. After White has not taken a drink for six months they congratulate each other. The following day White is found in the gutter.

The fourth role is that of the Patsy, or Dummy. In literature this is played by the delicatessen man who extends credit to White, gives him a sandwich on the cuff and perhaps a cup of coffee, without either persecuting him or trying to rescue him. In life this is more frequently played by White's mother, who gives him money and often sympathizes with him about the wife who does not understand him. In this aspect of the game, White is required to account in some plausible way for his need for money—by some project in which both pretend to believe, although they know what he is really going to spend most of the money for. Sometimes the Patsy slides over into another role, which is a helpful but not essential one: the Agitator, the "good guy" who offers supplies without even being asked for them: "Come have a drink with me (and you will go downhill faster)."

The ancillary professional in all drinking games is the bartender or liquor clerk. In the game "Alcoholic" he plays the fifth role, the Connection, the direct source of supply and who in a way is the most meaningful person in the life of any addict. The difference between the Connection and the other players is the difference between professionals and amateurs in any game: the professional knows when to stop. At a certain point a good bartender refuses to serve the Alcoholic, who is then left without any supplies unless he can locate a more indulgent Connection.

In the initial stages of "Alcoholic," the wife may play all three supporting roles: at midnight the Patsy, undressing him, making him coffee, and letting him beat up on her; in the morning the Persecutor, berating him for the evil of his ways; and in the evening the Rescuer, pleading with him to change them. In the later stages, due sometimes to organic deterioration, the Persecutor and the Rescuer can be dispensed with, but are tolerated if they are also willing to act as sources of supply. White will go to the Mission House and be rescued if he can get a free meal there; or he will stand for a scolding, amateur or professional, as long as he can get a handout afterward.

Present experience indicates that the *payoff* in "Alcoholic" (as is characteristic of games in general) comes from the aspect to which most investigators pay least attention. In the analysis of this game, drinking itself is merely an incidental pleasure having added advantages, the procedure leading up to the real culmination, which is the hangover. It is the same in the game of Schlemiel: the mess-making, which attracts the most attention, is merely a pleasure-giving way for White to lead to the crux, which is obtaining forgiveness from Black.

For the Alcoholic the hangover is not as much the physical pain as the psychological torment. The two favorite pastimes of drinking people are "Martini" (how many drinks, and how they were mixed) and "Morning After" ("Let me tell you about *my* hangover"). "Martini" is played, for the most part, by social drinkers; many alcoholics prefer a hard round of psychological "Morning After," and organizations such as A.A. offer them an unlimited opportunity for this.

Whenever one patient visited his psychiatrist after a binge, he would call himself all sorts of names; the psychiatrist said nothing. Later, recounting these visits in a therapy group, White said with smug satisfaction that it was the psychiatrist who had called him all those names. The main conversational interest of many alcoholics in the therapeutic situation is not their drinking, which they apparently mention mostly in deference to their persecutors, but their subsequent suffering. The transactional object of the drinking, aside from the personal pleasures it brings, is to set up a situation where the Child can be severely scolded not only by the internal

Parent but by any parental figures in the environment who are interested enough to oblige. (For a discussion of these ego states, please see Chapter 7.) Hence the therapy of this game should be concentrated not on the drinking but on the morning after, the self-indulgence in self-castigation. There is a type of heavy drinker, however, who does not have hangovers, and such people do not belong in the present category.

There are a variety of organizations involved in "Alcoholic," some of them national or even international in scope, others local. Many of them publish rules for the game. Nearly all of them explain how to play the role of Alcoholic: take a drink before breakfast, spend money allotted for other purposes, etc. They also explain the function of the Rescuer. Alcoholics Anonymous, for example, continues playing the actual game but concentrates on inducing the Alcoholic to take the role of Rescuer. Former Alcoholics are preferred because they know how the game goes, and hence are better qualified to play the supporting role than people who have never played before. Cases have been reported of a chapter of A.A. running out of Alcoholics to work on; whereupon the members resumed drinking, since there was no other way to continue the game in the absence of people to rescue.

There are also organizations devoted to improving the lot of the other players. Some put pressure on the spouses to shift their roles from Persecutor to Rescuer. The one which seems to come closest to the theoretical ideal of treatment deals with teenage offspring of alcoholics; these young people are encouraged to break away from the game itself, rather than merely shift their roles.

The psychological cure of an alcoholic also lies in getting him to stop playing the game altogether, rather than simply change from one role to another. In some cases this has been feasible, although it is a difficult task to find something else as interesting to the Alcoholic as continuing his game. Since he is classically afraid of intimacy, the substitute may have to be another game rather than a game-free relationship. Often so-called cured alcoholics are not very stimulating company socially, and possibly they feel a lack of excitement in their lives and are continually tempted to go back to their old ways. *The criterion of a true "game cure" is that the former Alcoholic should be able to drink socially without putting himself in jeopardy.* The usual "total abstinence" cure will not satisfy the game analyst.

It is apparent from the description of this game that there is a strong temptation for the Rescuer to play "I'm Only Trying to Help You"; for the

Persecutor to play "Look What You've Done to Me"; and for the Patsy to play "Good Joe." With the rise of rescue organizations which publicize the idea that alcoholism is a disease, alcoholics have been taught to play "Wooden Leg." ["What do you expect from a man with a wooden leg?"] The law, which takes a special interest in such people, tends to encourage this nowadays. The emphasis has shifted from the Persecutor to the Rescuer, from "I am a sinner" to "What do you expect from a sick man?" (part of the trend in modern thinking away from religion and toward science). From an existential point of view the shift is questionable, and from a practical point of view it seems to have done little to diminish the sale of liquor to heavy drinkers. Nevertheless, Alcoholics Anonymous is still for most people the best initiation in the therapy of overindulgence.

The reader will note that within the text of this quotation, I have highlighted a sentence which has created a veritable furor in the field of alcoholism: *"The criterion of a true "game cure" is that the former alcoholic should be able to drink socially without putting himself in jeopardy."* This statement has generated a lot of ill will from people who believe that alcoholism is an incurable disease. It implies that alcoholism is a game, not a disease, and that if an alcoholic gave up the game, he would be able to drink socially without putting himself in the danger of reverting to alcoholism. This is a radical statement indeed, but it must be carefully read. To many alcohol workers, especially those who have an allegiance to A.A., this statement is extremely disturbing and alarming. I have debated this issue far and wide, and I find that when I get a thoughtful rather than irrational response from one of these people, the issue becomes clearer. The feeling is that a person who has attained an uncertain sobriety may hear or read Berne's (or my) statements and derive from them a false hope which could precipitate a binge. I can well understand this concern. It is very valid because that danger is very real.

Berne does not mean to imply that alcoholics can continue to drink without putting themselves in jeopardy. By his definition, alcoholism is a game, and if you give up the game, you are no longer an alcoholic (something that A.A. claims is impossible). Accordingly, there is no suggestion that someone who has not come to the point where he is no longer alcoholic could or should be drinking socially or otherwise.

Furthermore, the word *socially* is very important word in this discussion. Social drinking is a specific form of drinking, and it excludes the kind of drinking that most people think of as social. Having a couple of cocktails before dinner, some wine with the meal, and a snifter of after-dinner liqueur, having six or seven drinks at a party or a six-pack of beer during a hot afternoon is not social drinking. Social drinking is a glass of wine during dinner or a drink before dinner or a couple of beers at a long party or a thimblefull of liqueur after a hearty meal. Social drinking is done for the taste of the alcohol and for the slight heady feeling that accompanies it in small amounts. What goes under the rubric of social drinking in this country is actually the first step—if not a more advanced stage—of alcoholism.

Finally, Berne's statement does seem to imply that a former alcoholic *has* to drink socially in order to prove that he's not an alcoholic anymore. Yet, I believe that all he meant was that the only way that an outsider can judge whether an alcoholic is really cured is if the alcoholic is able to drink socially.

In this light, therefore, Berne's statement can be rewritten: "Alcoholism is not an incurable illness, but a game; therefore it can be given up. One test of whether a person is no longer an alcoholic is if he drinks socially—that is, ceremonially—without embarking on a new cycle of drunkenness."

So much for Eric Berne's view. My own view on this matter derives from his view, but it is significantly different as well, and is expressed in the next chapter.

2

Can the Alcoholic Return to Social Drinking?

My answer to this question is of minor importance in my own work with alcoholics, yet I feel I have to answer it for the sake of the large number of people who are concerned with alcoholism and who take strong exception to my point of view. Many people object most vehemently to the mere suggestion that a person who was once an alcoholic can return to social drinking. These concerned people are usually connected with Alcoholics Anonymous.

Alcoholics Anonymous commands a great deal of respect from me because of its great success in dealing with alcoholism. Alcoholics Anonymous chapters meet frequently in virtually every city and town in the United States and are freely accessible to all people. Millions owe their sobriety to A.A. It works, and it is available to practically everybody at no cost. That is a remarkable achievement indeed.

However, the very factors that have made A.A. successful, have also caused it to become a dominating and sometimes overbearing force in the field of alcoholism. It is surely not the intention of the individual members and workers of A.A. to behave like religious fanatics who allow no thought that does not conform to dogma. Yet, A.A.'s ideology dominates the field of alcoholism. Alcoholics who are not attracted to A.A., feel like lost sheep who have strayed, outcasts from the fold. People who have drinking problems and who come in contact with the courts or other public institutions, but who are not willing to relate to A.A. will find themselves treated like heretics, and will have a great deal of difficulty getting help from people who can affect their lives. Alcoholism workers who do not accept A.A.'s total program will find that they cannot find work. Their own ideas or suggestions will not be welcome in clinics or other institutions. In short, A.A. is an organization which, because of its unequivocal success in working with alcoholics, has become a monopoly and a repressive influence in the field. People will find it difficult to function effectively as alcohol workers unless they are willing to bend to A.A.'s will.

The point of view which I present in this book is a different approach to alcoholism. Although I agree (largely) with A.A., I disagree with some of its specific beliefs, because the evidence I see compels me to do so. Some former alcoholics who have remained sober for at least a year while actively involved in therapy with me have been able to go back to social drinking. Almost every alcoholic I have worked with has wanted at some point or another to test his or her ability to drink socially. Alcoholics who have wanted to run this test while in therapy with me have fallen into one of three groups:

People in one group—the largest by far—discover that they are unable to drink alcohol at any level, and that the inevitable result of having even one drink, is that ultimately their drinking goes out of control and becomes harmful.

People in the second group discover, as they experiment with social drinking, that they are uncomfortably drawn to alcohol, that their intake increases slowly and imperceptibly, and that their thoughts become more and more involved with alcohol in that pattern we are all so familiar with. Their drinking becomes "controlled alcoholic drinking." But the members of this group decide that drinking is not for them and stop drinking without incident or harmful aftereffects.

People in the third and smallest group discover that alcohol is no longer an obsession. It no longer becomes a progressive compulsion, and they are able to simply take an occasional, enjoyable, social drink without any dire consequences. My estimate of the size of this group agrees with Armor's findings [1] of between 10 and 20 percent of all alcoholics in treatment.

I believe that people who have once been powerless in the face of alcohol can change their lives. Helping them become the kind of people who can look at the forces that affect their lives and can decide what they want to do, what to let into their lives, what to put into their mouths, is the aim of my work, and I believe that I've been successful in helping many people achieve that goal. I believe people can develop power over their lives. I've seen people exercise that power over their alcoholism—a few of them to the point of drinking socially.

Most people who have succeeded in becoming ex-alcoholics while working with me have power over alcohol and will not let it destroy their lives. Most of those people discover that even though they haven't had a drink for many years, alcohol continues to hold a strange physical and mental fascination which increases greatly if they have even one drink. But those people stay away from alcohol without incident or difficulty.

I am fully convinced that people who have been habitual drinkers for many years have a strong tendency to return to this pattern. The past habits are like old ruts on a road; they remain a part of you, and once you fall into them, they are very hard to get out of. In this respect, alcoholics are no different from people who are addicted to cigarettes. Drinking and smoking become automatic behaviors: once you take step number one, step number two tends to follow, step number three becomes easier, and step number four becomes almost inevitable.

In his excellent monograph, *The Emergent Comprehensive Concept of Alcoholism,*[2] James Milam points out that evidence indicates that alcoholics experience certain improvements in mood and mental and motor skills when drinking which are not experienced by nonalcoholics. This effect, combined with the pressures of habit, would make the attempt at social drinking extremely difficult to control; people who were once alcoholics are playing with fire when they try to drink again.

I take it for granted that sooner or later, people who have been in therapy with me, who have not been drinking, and feel strong, are going to ask what I think about their trying to drink socially. My usual response is one of great caution. I explain that I believe it is risky, but I cannot say that there is an automatic, inevitable, fatal, consequence from social drinking. It simply does not reflect my experience and I have a contract of complete honesty with my clients.

Occasionally, former alcoholics simply return to social drinking and continue to do so without incident. Anyone who wishes to is free to argue that they were not alcoholics to begin with. While that seems like a self-serving argument, it may actually be true. What is important is dealing with each person's experience with alcohol separately, rather than lumping all alcoholics together.

One more point needs to be dealt with. I have heard it said repeatedly that by writing and speaking about even the remotest possibility of drinking for former alcoholics, I am endangering the sobriety of the tens of thousands who would go down the drain if they tried this method. I recognize that a person who is an alcoholic and who has been sober for years might pick up this book and after reading it might have a drink, and then go from there into an alcoholic binge. It is not my intention to create that situation, but I must tell the truth, and that is more important than shielding an unknown human being from the possible potential risk that my ideas might provoke.

In the history of ideas, many valid ideas have been considered dangerous. But ideas are primarily correct or erroneous, rather than safe or dangerous. I would like my ideas to have some breathing space next to A.A.'s ideas. After all, I am a mere mouse among a herd of A.A. elephants, and any danger that my small voice might generate could be quickly dealt with by the massive power of A.A.'s views.

My main point is not that alcoholics can return to social drinking, but that alcoholism can be healed. Only time will tell who is right, and I'm sure we will find, in the end, that neither I nor A.A., are completely right or wrong, but that the truth lies somewhere in some unexpected middle.

3

Roles and Games

In *Games People Play*,[1] Eric Berne pointed out that a game is based on transactions which originate from the different roles of the game. Each game has different roles, and he noted that the game of Alcoholic had five: the Alcoholic, the Persecutor, the Rescuer, the Patsy, and the Connection. It has recently become clear to me that Alcoholic has only three, rather than five, roles: the Persecutor, Rescuer, and the Victim. Berne's Patsy is basically a Victim, and the Connection is a business person who does not play the game but profits from it. When alcohol is supplied by a friend or relative, this is usually done from the Patsy (Victim) or from the Patsy-soon-to-become-a-Rescuer role rather than from the Connection role. This very helpful simplification of the game roles was made possible by the discovery of the Drama Triangle by Stephen Karpman.[2]

Karpman perceived that of the many roles and switches between roles which are common in games, three main roles and the switches between them are at the root of all dramatic developments in life. He arranged the three roles of Rescuer, Persecutor, and Victim in a triangle to symbolize the switching that occurs between them. The drama triangle is a brilliant schematic of the futile and mechanical merry-go-round in which people are trapped when they play games.

Life can be lived genuinely, or it can be lived as a stage play in which everything is make-believe, although it may reflect real life. The three dramatic game roles—the Persecutor, Rescuer, and Victim—are the melodramatic simplifications of real life. We see ourselves as generous Rescuers of grateful or ungrateful Victims. We see ourselves as righteous Persecutors of the wicked and as Victims of the wicked Persecutor. Playing any of these roles, we lose perspective of the realities that confront us. We simplify the complexities of real life and ignore reality, like actors on a stage who know that their lives are not real but must pretend that they are, to put on a good show.

Figure 1 The Drama Triangle

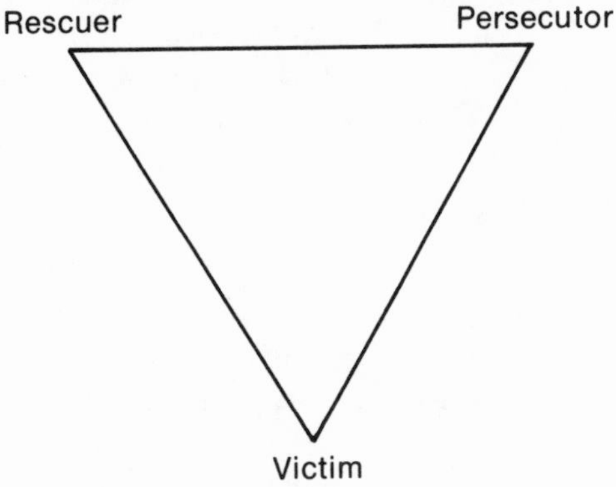

Rescuer — Persecutor — Victim

Especially dramatic are the sudden changes which are caused by the switches between the roles. We never remain long in any of them: the playboy falls in love and gets jilted; the loving wife ruins her husband; the oppressive boss becomes a downtrodden worker; the doting parent becomes a victim of her children; the criminal is paroled and forgiven by society.

Nowhere is the drama triangle more clearly illustrated than in the game of Alcoholism.

Consider the following typical case report:

Mr. S. white, male, 39, married, three children, employed, comes to the alcoholism clinic seeking help. He fears that he is going to lose his job. His wife has threatened to leave him. He has just received a drunk-driving ticket. He is shaky, contrite, eager to be helped. He readily agrees that he is an alcoholic, that his drinking is out of control, and that he needs to stop drinking completely. He signs up for therapy sessions once a week.

At the first therapy meeting, he discusses his drinking history, describes his relationship with his wife and family and speaks about his work as a draftsman. He says he loves his family and enjoys his job and swears that he has stopped drinking once and for all.

At the second meeting, Mr. S. is quite changed. He seems confident, hasn't had anything to drink for fourteen days, is cheerful and full of confidence. He had his day in court, pled guilty to drunk driving, and was given a suspended sentence if he would participate in therapy. His job seems secure, and his wife and children are happy with his changes. He thanks the therapist for his help.

During the next several therapy meetings, Mr. S. seems to be in very good shape, reports his progress, and has nothing in particular to discuss. He talks about his childhood, his dreams, his problems at work and with his car. He doesn't feel that there is anything worth discussing in his own life at this time.

After a month of therapy, the therapist becomes a little suspicious of Mr. S.'s behavior and attempts to probe into some of the developments in his life? Is he getting along at work? Is he depressed? How is his family life? Mr. S. becomes defensive and says that he is convinced his problem is solved. He does not plan to have a drink ever again. He is coming to therapy only because it is a condition of probation and because he promised his wife.

The next week, Mr. S. misses his session. That evening the therapist is awakened at 2:00 A.M. by an emergency call (relayed by the therapist's answering service) from Mrs. S. Evidently Mr. S. has been drinking and has just left the house and driven away after a fight with her. While Mrs. S. is talking on the phone, Mr. S. returns and wants to know whom she is speaking to. When he finds out that she is speaking to the therapist, he becomes even angrier. At first he refuses to come to the phone, but eventually does and promises to stop drinking and go to bed.

Just as the therapist is falling asleep again, the phone rings. Mrs. S., scared and angry, reports that Mr. S. has hit her and has left the house again. She seems to be blaming the therapist for the situation. The therapist tries to smooth the waters and goes back to bed. The next day at the clinic, Mr. S. appears bleary-eyed and shaky; he has missed work for a couple of days. Things are worse than when he first came. This time the therapist notes certain erratic behavior in Mr. S. and comes to the decision that Mr. S.'s alcoholism is a cover for a latent psychosis. He refers Mr. S. to the clinic's physician, who prescribes Thorazine and Antabuse. Mr. S. doesn't want to take Antabuse, but is happy to take Thorazine and to get some vitamin shots. He promises to stop drinking and to come back to the group and resume therapy.

At the staff meeting the therapist and the clinic physician discuss Mr. S.'s case. They are both cynical and somewhat bitter. The therapist decides to drop Mr. S. from therapy if he misses any more meetings, and the physician jokes: "I bet you a lunch at the Chinese restaurant that his sobriety doesn't last more than six weeks." (He would have won the bet had anybody taken him up on it.)

This is a typical story, which has surely repeated itself around the country thousands of times. On the surface, it seems to be real as life. In fact, it is a melodrama or soap opera. It is melodrama, rather than a drama, because it isn't of sufficient epic proportions. But, like a play, it appears to have all of the characteristics of real life. The roles of Victim, Persecutor, and Rescuer are defined, and Mr. S. moves from one to the other with ease; first, the pathetic Victim to the therapist's Rescuer, next, the Persecutor who beats his wife and harasses the therapist, and then again the hopeless Victim.

The therapist is equally involved in the melodrama—first as the helpful Rescuer, next as the confused Victim in Mr. S.'s charade, next as the Victim of Mr. and Mrs. S.'s persecution, then eventually the Persecutor as he decides to drop Mr. S. from his group and refers him to the physician. The physician plays his part as the Rescuer and eventually joins the therapist in subtle Persecution as they decide that Mr. S. is a hopeless case.

This decision has dire consequences for Mr. S., who now has a new bad rating added to his diagnosis. Until his latest bout, his diagnosis was listed as "alcohol addiction (300.2)." He now has a new number added: "296.9 (unspecified major affective disorder)." To any future health workers looking at his file, the fact that there is a "two hundred" attached to Mr. S.'s diagnosis means: "Warning! Psychotic: Medicate and don't bother." The major negative consequence of this is not that he will probably not be offered individual psychotherapy any longer (that could actually be a blessing in disguise) but that he will be treated with that special subtle contempt reserved for those who are labeled "psychotic."

Mrs. S. is involved, too. First she threatens to leave him after months of attempting to Rescue him. Later she becomes the Patsy/Victim again, when she believes he is going to straighten out. Then, when he starts drinking again, she becomes angry, persecutes him and the therapist, and so on and so forth, endlessly. Thus, everyone in the alcoholic's circle plays one of the three roles sooner or later.

Games are dramatizations of life rather than life itself; yet the players of the game roles feel that their roles are real. The Rescuer feels that he is truly helping the alcoholic, and the alcoholic feels that he is a helpless Victim of alcoholism. When either of them becomes a Persecutor, they believe that they have a valid complaint and that their anger is justified. They don't see how temporary the roles are and how circumstantial their participation is in it. In short, they live the role as if it were real at the time. However, if one is not playing the game, one can see that the Victim is not really as helpless as he feels, the Rescuer is not really helping, and the Persecutor does not really have a valid complaint—and that they all know it, deep inside. Thus, the whole drama, when seen in this light, is basically phony—and it is necessary for an observer who wants to understand the situation to know this so as to not get caught up in it.

Alcoholism is a game in a nongenuine life script. Anyone who wishes to really help an alcoholic needs to stay outside the melodrama. This can be accomplished by refusing to play any of the roles—Rescuer, Persecutor or Victim—and pursuing the realities of alcoholism instead.

Why People Play Games

Games are played for motives and payoffs not readily obvious to most participants or even observers. But if what seems obvious (the game roles) isn't the whole story, then what *is* going on? What is going on is that Mr. S. is becoming hopelessly addicted to alcohol, that Mrs. S. is getting fed up and hates him, that his children are afraid of him, that his boss has already decided to fire him, and that his therapist has given up on him. Mr. S. is terrified, feels rejected and alone, hurt and angry, and none of this is being acknowledged or discussed. Instead, Mr. S. and his circle play Alcoholic over and over.

People need a certain amount of social contact. They want to be with other people. They want to spend time talking to one another. They want to have loving relationships with friends, their children, spouses, or lovers. People are hungry for what Eric Berne called "strokes."

A stroke is a unit of human recognition. Human recognition, affection, love, admiration, nurturing, physical contact, are essential for the psychological—if not the physical—survival of human beings, just as is good food, clean air, water, and shelter, and all the other basic necessities of life. There is a scarcity of the kind of human interaction which generates positive human recognition in a simple, straightforward way. Because of this scarcity, people resort to other ways of getting strokes. Strokes can be given and taken freely, they can be obtained in honest barter, they can be bought, or they can be ripped off. Games are devious, subtle manipulations to get the strokes or recognition, affection and attention that people need from each other. When looking at the alcoholic and his circle playing the game, it is important to realize that even though the roles that are being played are constantly changing, one thing remains constant: all of the people in the game are involved in a series of transactions which produce much-needed strokes.

Some of the strokes aren't as pleasant and as satisfying as they might be. Human interaction includes not only straightforward nurturing, loving, appreciative, gentle strokes, but also angry, demanding, impatient, judgmental, tense, anxious strokes. Unfortunately, games are much more productive of the negative than of the positive. When people play games they have given up their hope of having direct loving interactions, and are opting for an alternative (playing games) which they are more familiar with, but which usually ends badly.

Most games are started with the best of intentions: the Alcoholic wants to have some fun, the Rescuer wants to help (the Patsy/Rescuer wants to trust), and the Persecutor wants to make sure that justice is done. After a few transactions, however, the plot inevitably goes sour, there is a switch, and the situation becomes ugly, unpleasant, and bitter.

Still, interaction does take place, and the players do get something out of the game. Even though the outcome is not as pleasant as it could be, there is a certain amount of human contact and strokes derived that makes playing the game worth the trouble. Because of this, people who don't know how to get strokes in a direct way will repeatedly approach the problem of stroke-hunger by playing games and, unless a direct way is shown and demonstrated to them, they will go back to the game approach because it is better than getting no strokes at all. People want love, but if it isn't available, they'll settle for anything: strokes or pokes.

Ironically, in addition to getting strokes, games help avoid intimacy as well. Intimacy is the most direct, open, sincere, and loving form of strokes. Most people, even though they fundamentally want this kind of stroke, are worried about and afraid of them. We don't easily open up to others for that kind of extremely loving interaction, and we don't really think that we want those kind of strokes from most people. We tend to be cautious about whom we relate to in such an intense way and reserve those kinds of intimate strokes for our romantic, sexual relationships. In other words, there are certain kinds of strokes we don't want from most people, and when it appears that we are being threatened with that kind of direct approach we often cut it off.

This situation can be easily understood if we compare it with food. Most of us are accustomed to a certain kind of diet which includes lots of junk food. Thus, many people who eat regularly are undernourished although they overeat. Under these circumstances, they can be constantly hungry (and overweight) and seek ways to satisfy this hunger. Yet if offered a truly nutritious meal, they might not enjoy its taste and might put it aside in favor of the less nutritious but more familiar junk food. Similarly, people who are hungry for strokes will continually seek and consume strokes which aren't necessarily healthy—hostile, anxious, negative strokes—and will actually refuse the more intimate, direct, loving strokes that might be offered and available to them.

Games, therefore, provide strokes which are mostly negative and fend off positive, intimate strokes. Because games are essentially bad habits based on poor learning experiences, they can be stopped. The pursuit of positive, intimate strokes can be substituted in the place of games.

Let's look at three alcoholic games: "Drunk and Proud," "Lush," and "Wino."

4

Drunk and Proud

As the title of this game implies, the D&P alcoholic is a drinker, and proud of it. For the D&P player, who is most often a man, alcoholism is a way of asserting himself, by stimulating people around him who are willing to play the game into behaving either as foolish Victims/Patsies (who believe every lie, go along with every absurd proposal, and continually come back for more), or as Persecutors who are angry, mean, intolerant, and show with their behavior that they are basically no good—certainly no better than the alcoholic himself.

D&P is often played by freewheeling salesmen and business executives and working men as Alcoholics and their wives as Rescuers and Persecutors. The game punishes the wife for her dominating, condescending, nagging, and possessive attitudes. When drunk, a D&P player can make sexy moves with the secretaries, gamble away his paycheck at the poker table, and stay out with the boys without paying any dues. When his wife finally gets to him next morning and reproaches him, he smilingly apologizes: "Oh, boy, I feel terrible about this, honey. I'll try to be good from now on." The wife now has two choices: either she accepts the apology, thereby becoming a dummy (Rescuer/Patsy), or she rejects the "contrite" apology and becomes merciless and bitchy (Persecutor).

The D&P player doesn't ordinarily miss any work—at least not more than anybody else does—and manages to keep everything going fairly well. He seldom hangs around the house to get drunk since drinking is only an avenue of misbehavior of another kind. He drinks and drives, drinks and gambles, drinks and beats his wife, drinks and lies—in fact, drinking is the continuous excuse and constant companion for every other form of mischief. If anyone tries to be helpful and speaks to him about his "drinking problem," he will get angry, supercilious, and extremely defensive, and argue that he drinks for the taste of good liquor, that it is not harming him, that he can stop anytime he wants to, that it is necessary to drink to get ahead in his work, and so on and so forth. In fact, he will give all of the arguments that neutralize the assumption he has a drinking problem.

The D&P player does not believe and will not admit that he is an alcoholic. Thus, he almost never finds his way to a psychotherapist's office on his own. When he does, usually because his wife has threatened to divorce him, or because a judge or probation officer sent him there, he is likely to engage the therapist in the game as the Rescuer. Any therapist who misses this point and is willing to undertake therapy with a D&P player, without a contract or clear-cut therapy agreement (see Chapter 13), or thinks that discussing childhood experiences or analyzing dreams will be of any advantage whatsoever, will find, as she becomes increasingly confident that the therapy is "making progress," that she is exposing herself to an inevitable and monumental disappointment.

Trying to help a reluctant D&P alcoholic with his drinking problem is probably the most frustrating and unrewarding experience that any helpful person could possibly have. It is essentially a hopeless effort, and it is in connection with D&P players that it becomes totally obvious that no therapist should undertake therapy with an alcoholic without a contract. To illustrate the frustration of trying to work with a D&P alcoholic without a contract, let me tell you about the case of the Winking Patient.

Mr. Lavat, a 36-year-old D&P player, was preceded by his lover of many years who came to see me, wanting to discuss what she could do about him. This was many years ago, in the days when I was still willing to discuss with their partners what could be done to help alcoholics. Nowadays, I know better. If someone who has an alcoholic in her life needs and wants to speak to me, I generally decline discussion of what can be done to help the alcoholic, but rather insist that we discuss what can be done to help the advice seeker.

But with Mr. Lavat, I suggested, after some discussion, that she threaten to leave him as a maneuver to get him to come into therapy.

She did, and consequently, one sunny morning, I was pleased to have him call me for an appointment. From the beginning, Mr. Lavat dealt with me in a jovial, friendly, "Hi, Doc, how-ya-doing, what's new with you" manner. Inexperienced as I was then, I accepted his coming to see me at face value and assumed that he was interested in doing something about his alcoholism. We started the usual exploration of the "reasons" for his drinking. He was talkative and interesting, and we worked well together. He stopped drinking and continued to be sober as the weeks passed. One day as I met him in the waiting room, he added a wink to his usual friendly manner. I noticed this but didn't comment on it, although it gave me a very clear-cut feeling of discomfort. Every week from then on, Mr. Lavat would meet me with a wink. This continued for several months, during which he continued to make "progress" and remain sober. I never challenged the meaning of his winks and continued to do "therapy."

Then, quite unexpectedly, I found out that Mr. Lavat had been drinking for several weeks. It turned out that at approximately the same time when he started winking at me, he also began drinking and had continued to drink between appointments. He probably stayed away from alcohol the nights before our sessions and managed to hide the fact that he was drinking. Because of my inexperience, I did not pick up the clues, which would not escape me today. Conned in such an obvious way, I felt quite foolish and realized that I had been playing Patsy in the game of Alcoholic. Mr. Lavat never returned for another therapy session, and I learned a number of valuable lessons:

Never do therapy without a contract.

Always inquire about the client's drinking and maintain a reasonable level of suspicion and paranoia about it.

Finally: A winking client is usually up to no good.

This last rule refers to alcoholics who wink and use other subtle and humorous gestures to tip off the therapist to the fact that he is in danger of being made a fool.

Alcoholics are difficult clients to begin with, even if they really want therapy. D&P alcoholics are usually simply not interested in being therapy clients at all, and most of the therapy done with them is a waste of time. A therapist who finds himself involved in "doing therapy" with a D&P alcoholic whose involvement he suspects of being insincere should probably take the first opportunity to suggest that therapy be discontinued. "I think you are right—you probably aren't an alcoholic. Maybe you are wasting your time in therapy. Let's stop in a couple of weeks." If he accepts discontinuation, the situation is clear: the therapy was part of a game. If he declines and wishes to continue, they can then proceed to make a contract.

Whenever a D&P player goes to a physician because of severe illness caused by drinking, his attitude is roughly "Okay, doc, here we go again. Just give me the ole shot in the arms and the pills. My! Have I got a dilly of a hangover, haha, see you 'round." This attitude is disconcerting to physicians, who think of alcoholism in terms of illness and fail to understand that alcoholism is a game and that the hangover is a part of it.

As Berne points out, the hangover, with its agonies, is an essential aspect of the game. In it, the alcoholic's pain absolves him of deserved anger and punishment for all of his misdeeds. Any judgmental or disapproving word from a helper will be seen as unfair and probably be answered with hurt indignation. "You wouldn't hit a sick man, would you, doc? . . . How can you be so cruel? Can't you see I'm dying—you call yourself a doctor?" This typical situation exemplifies the physician's dilemma. He's left with one of three choices: to be a Persecutor, to be a Rescuer, or, if he is less scrupulous, to simply be a businesslike Connection to drugs and vitamins whose only concern is making a living.

D&P alcoholics are seldom interested in hurting themselves irreversibly, since their main payoff comes from the guiltless expression of their anger, and sexual naughtiness. When a D&P player begins to feel the ravages of alcoholism, he often stops drinking. This may take a number of years involving a series of initially unsuccessful attempts, but there are many people who were once alcoholics who have sobered up and haven't been drunk or had a drink for many, many years. They probably were D&P alcoholics who eventually decided to stop expressing their angry and sexual impulses via alcohol. It is as if D&P alcoholism is a behavior pattern of the impulsive younger years, which, as the person becomes more mature and thoughtful, is likely to be given up because of its inappropriateness. This is what distinguishes D&P from the game of Lush, which will be discussed in the next chapter. While the D&P is angry and rebellious, the Lush is depressed and needy.

D&P is a game of rebellion, a game in which a person who is being told that he is not O.K. turns the tables on his accusers and proves *them* not O.K. It is one of a family of games, played on different territories, in which people rebel against the judgments of "holier than thou" players (soberer than thou, better than thou, lefter than thou, etc.) D&P is related to High and Proud, described in *Games Alcoholics Play* as the game of the student antiwar movement of the Sixties. To the extent that all the games of this family are manifestations of reasonable rebelliousness against oppressive judgments by others, it is an expression of a healthy aspect of the person, even though in some of its aspects it is a damaging activity.

In order to be helpful to any player in this family of games, it is necessary for the helper to recognize the healthy aspects interwoven in the maneuvers of the players and separate them from those which are damaging. It is useful to remember that positive social movements have developed from this kind of rebelliousness. Black is beautiful, gay is O.K., the women's movement, the spirit of '76 and, one might guess, all of the movements for liberation have begun with people who rebelled against the judgments made by society. In the early phases of such movements, this rebellion, which is quite justified, is always vague, impulsive, irrational, and often self-damaging, as well as downright destructive of self and others.

I believe that the D&P player's rebellion is somewhat justified. I can sympathize with his anger at being called incurably ill, at being encouraged to drink, on one hand, and judged for his drinking on the other, at being dealt with in a supercilious and unstraight manner, at having his addiction exploited by bar and liquor-store owners and the alcohol industry.

The D&P player wants to be proud of himself. The problem is that he is choosing drunkenness as a subject of his pride. To be adequately helpful, one needs to be identified with his desire for pride and separate it from the drunkenness. The D&P player feels that he is justified and O.K. in his behavior, and he certainly is not going to listen to anyone who says that he is not. The therapist's only hope is to agree with the D&P player that he is O.K. and to get him to examine his alcoholic behavior, and recognize how destructive of self and others it is. This attitude is one of the major contributions of TA to psychotherapy: that the therapist always approaches the client with the attitude that he is O.K. and that it is only his behavior which is being scrutinized (and that only at his invitation after he chooses to do so.)

All of this may imply that I am saying we should not judge alcoholics and that we should leave it up to them to do something about their problem. This is my view, but only up to the point where the alcoholic hurts no one but himself. When his behavior damages others, it clearly must be responded to. But the response should not be therapy, unless it is requested. The response to irresponsible, destructive behavior should be fair, swift justice through the courts. When the damage, as is so often the case, results in pain and hardship for relatives, friends, and even strangers, the response should be a fair one—such as rejection, anger, or an ultimatum. But not therapy, unless he seeks it.

Alcoholism is not an illness or a crime, but it can lead to both. When it includes illness, it should be referred to a physician for treatment of that illness. When it includes crime, it should be referred to the courts. When it includes neither, which is most often the case, it should be left to the alcoholic himself to choose what to do. The only thing we can do to help is not to allow ourselves to play the game as Victims, Rescuers, or Persecutors and to be honest and straightforward instead.

One of the big bones of contention in the therapy of alcoholism is whether any one player is in fact an alcoholic. D&P players, especially, hotly deny that they are alcoholics, and often take offense when the suggestion is made. The following are typical examples of conversations with D&P players. Each one represents an attempt to make the point that he is an alcoholic and gives the suspected alcoholic's easy rebuttal of that point.

The Blunt Approach

"Mr. Smith, as far as I'm concerned, you're an alcoholic."

"Well, that may be so. I've often wondered about it. Sometimes I think I am, but actually, come to think of it, I don't think so."

The Sneaky Approach

"Mr. Smith, do you think you're an alcoholic?" (Implying that he is.)

"No, actually, I don't think so. An alcoholic is somebody who can't control his drinking. But I control my drinking. I never drink before noon, and I can stop anytime. I never get a hangover. I'm a heavy drinker, but I hold my liquor very well, and I don't have a problem with it."

The Argumentative Approach

"Yes, but last weekend you had a drink first thing in the morning."

"Yes, but that was just because it was so hot and I needed a cold beer."

"Yes, but you looked pretty sick to me Monday morning."

"Yes, but that's because I had the beginning of the flu. Actually, I had a large glass of Hi-C with vodka, which is the perfect remedy for colds."

"Yes, but you were staggering pretty badly when you came out of the party the other day."

"Yes, but a cup of coffee sobered me right up. I got home okay, didn't I?"

These examples are given to show that as long as one tries to prove the alcoholic wrong or not O.K., very little will be accomplished. The point is not to prove him not O.K., the point is to enlist him in an examination of the destructive aspects of his behavior. And that, of course, cannot be done unless the alcoholic asks for help, at which time he may be ready to examine his behavior carefully. If he asks the question, "Am I an alcoholic?" my answer is, "If you really want to know, I'm going to ask you two questions. If you answer either of them "yes," then I believe you are an alcoholic. Do you want to try?"

I always make sure not to ask the questions unless the person is very interested and I feel that the answers are going to be honest and clear.

My first question is: "Do you feel that you have lost control over your drinking? For instance, do you sometimes drink more than you want to, or do you sometimes drink at times when you don't want to drink? If the answer is yes, then you are an alcoholic."

The second question is: "Do you feel that your drinking is harming you in any way? At work? Financially? In relationships? In any other way?" If so, you are an alcoholic. How severe an alcoholic depends on how out of control and damaging your drinking is, but if the answer is "yes," then you are somewhere on the road from mild to severe alcoholism.

I am very earnest about not diagnosing alcoholism except in this way. I'm not in the business of telling people that they are this, that, or the other thing. I have never been able to help anyone who didn't sincerely ask for help and who wasn't willing to recognize and analyze his own behavior honestly. Nowhere is the necessity to enlist the client's sincere involvement more important than in the therapy of alcoholism and other drug and chemical abuse.

5

Lush

Before I describe the game of Lush, I want to explain that the only reason to divide the alcoholic game into different subgames is to point out that all alcoholic behavior is not one and the same; all alcoholism does not come from the same personal motivation and have the same historical origins. TA (transactional analysis) has been accused—and rightfully so, at times—of unnecessarily picking apart human behavior and contributing cute titles to essentially banal distinctions. In this case, however, I believe that the distinctions between the three alcoholic games reflect real and important differences in alcoholic behavior, and that they are useful in understanding alcoholism. I am not providing these categories in order for people to be able to prove how smart they are by making quick shot-from-the-hip diagnoses of each other. I shudder when I hear people discuss other human beings with the easy abandon that is possible when using TA (or any other) labels. If you are going to use these ideas, please use them thoughtfully, respectfully, and, above all, don't use them as clubs with which to accuse others of "gamey" behavior or as amateur-shrinks-with-the-latest-word.

The game of Lush has the same basic motivation as D&P or any other drug-abuse game. It is an attempt to solve the difficulty of living through the use of a chemical. In the case of Lush, however, the specific feeling of the player is one of depression and resignation, rather than one of rebellion, as it is in D&P. In North America, Lush is most often played by middle-aged suburban wives, or downtrodden, hard-working, white-collar employees. It is also played by aging male homosexuals, by Native Americans, and, in general, by people who, for one reason or another, are under a heavy load of oppression to which they have resigned themselves. The despair and hopelessness associated with their condition is dealt with by using alcohol as a sedative and mood elevator which gets them high, helps them forget their troubles, and makes life's daily difficulties bearable. Whenever the Lush is played, it is played in response to some sort of deprivation: whether it be sexual deprivation, loneliness, hunger, joblessness, or some other kind of hardship.

In its typically white, middle-class, North American version, Lush is usually played by a housewife with a partner (usually a man) for whom it is difficult to give strokes in a classically sexist couple arrangement. The alcoholic's continual drinking is to the partner's advantage, since as long as the drinking continues, his own emotional deficiencies and incapacities to be loving—which are his contribution to the game—will not be exposed. As long as the alcoholic drinks, the partner preserves the appearance of blamelessness, while of course both know that this is not true. Characteristically, the husband of a Lush player comes home late from work, anxious and drained, and avoids loving and sexual intimacy with the alcoholic. In order to get some attention, the Lush player uses a common maneuver in such cases: making a mess of some sort.

There are a number of other games, all of which share making a mess in order to get some strokes; this game is often played by children and their harried parents. Often the disinterested, unloving partner comes home to a drunken wife who has not cleaned the house and failed to prepare dinner. He may try to ignore her drunkenness, but this can be done only for so long. Sooner or later he will fall into the Persecuting role, calling her names, perhaps going out to eat alone, or even beating her. Or he may become the Rescuer, have long discussions with her about her drinking problem, take her out to dinner, or perform some other "helpful" maneuver, which he hopes will change the situation. But either way, the facts of his unlovingness and the dreariness of her life remain, and the reasons for the drinking remain.

Because Lush players react to strokes, it is customary for them to stop drinking temporarily and to make considerable progress when any kind of therapy or helping effort begins—whether it be Alcoholics Anonymous, a new, sympathetic physician, a brand-new friendship or a psychotherapist. Almost any kind of change will bring about a temporary, apparent improvement in the Lush's drinking. But because this improvement is a response to the increased strokes that come with a new relationship, the improvement is only temporary.

In the case of the psychotherapist, the progress may be cut short just as the therapist thinks the client is well enough to leave therapy. Clearly, since the client's progress was based on strokes from the therapist, it becomes important for the client to remain in therapy—something that can easily be accomplished by going back to drinking. Therefore, a therapist who is unaware of this pattern, will be caught in a situation where basically he is replacing—usually for a fee, and usually not in a wholly satisfactory way—strokes that the client is not getting in his or her intimate relationships. Commonly, the therapist will experience an intensified demand for strokes, on the one hand, and a relapse of the drinking every time the strokes are either withdrawn or not forthcoming in the amounts needed by the client. The same seesaw of improvement and relapse characterizes the relationships of Lush alcoholics with friends and relatives.

While D&P is a gregarious game, Lush is a solitary one. Often the Lush player drinks at home. However, on occasion, once under the influence of alcohol, the Lush player will leave the house to find a sexual contact wherever available. This is a shocking experience to Lush's partner, since often a middle-class woman will go to a working-class bar where she hooks up and sleeps with an unknown truck driver or sailor.

This example also shows how alcohol works. The woman who would never consider having sex with a stranger while she was sober, does so in a blackout. Blackout is a phenomenon in which the alcoholic, after having done a number of things, many of which are totally opposed to his moral values, will forget having done them. That is not to say that during the blackout the alcoholic is unconscious or unaware, but only that later, when sober, he doesn't remember what he did. This illustrates how alcohol works: First, it knocks out the Parent ego state, that is the moral inhibitions; next it knocks out the Adult, the rational aspect and the ego state that would remember what has been done; then the Child is free to do as it pleases. If the drinking continues, then the Child may be knocked out next and the person will be unconscious. But in the Parentless and Adultless state of the free Child, the Lush is able to go directly to those things he needs and wants—the strokes and sexual gratification, which he can't get at home and which he cannot obtain unless he wipes out his Parent and Adult with alcohol.

Unlike D&P, which tends to be a two- or three-person game, Lush tends to involve many persons: doctors, social workers, therapists, friends, and neighbors. D&P tends to be a game that involves people as Persecutors, while Lush tends to involve people as Rescuers. But this tendency is deceptive because people who play a game, play all the roles in it, sooner or later. Even though the Lush player tends to seem to be a Victim looking for a Rescuer, he will play the Persecutor role and the Rescuer roles as well—if ever so subtly. For example, the Lush may present herself to the therapist as needing help and being powerless and unable to do anything about her drinking. That is the Victim looking for a Rescuer. But if the therapist is inexperienced enough to indulge in a Rescue, this is likely to produce angry feelings in the Victim. Then, in time, the alcoholic will persecute the therapist in some way. One favored way Lush players persecute their therapists is to get drunk and thus prove the therapist to be ineffectual. Of course, the therapist may in fact be ineffectual, but the therapist who in addition is playing the game will feel the brunt of his incompetence hit him over the head because the alcoholic-turned-Persecutor will make sure that it hurts. More subtly, the Lush player will tend to take up more than her share of the time allotted in group, and yet fail to do any work outside of the therapy hour. If pressured, she will comply, but grudgingly, and not really work at it. This reluctant resistance comes from a sulking resentment against the therapist, which becomes a subtle form of Persecution.

Similarly, the Lush will play Rescuer to other group members or other alcoholics in A.A. or be very solicitous of the therapist, concerned about his health, inquire about his family, and protect him from her own anger and resentment by keeping it covered and underground. All of this will mask the fact that the reason why the Lush drinks has a lot to do with being deprived of strokes. The game, well played, provides the alcoholic with lots of strokes in the only way she knows how to get them.

6

Wino

Two major qualities characterize the game of Wino. First: the game is always part of a self-destructive life-script because it is played "for keeps." A person who plays the game of Wino is willing to include, as a part of the game, the permanent destruction of his body tissue. His game is part of a self-destructive script. Second: Wino is an institutional game, involving the institutions of the neighborhood, county, and state. The Wino becomes involved with the police, the courts, the jails, the public health system, and the oppressive crush of the inner city. As a resident of the city slums, he becomes the victim of slumlords and merchants, street crime, and real estate redevelopment schemes.

In the game of Wino, the alcoholic gains strokes by making himself physically ill. He is willing to sacrifice his body integrity to the point of putting his survival on the line, which forces others to take notice, either as Persecutors or Rescuers. Under these circumstances, those who come to his aid as Rescuers basically facilitate his progress toward the soup kitchen or jail, where he will be fed and sheltered, or to a clinic, where he will be given tranquilizers and nursing care. In any case, the Wino is physically devastated and therefore entitled to some kind of help. With every renewed game, the alcoholic obtains the confirmation for his Victim status.

It's pretty clear that unless he is at death's door, the Wino player will be mistreated and ignored; only under the most extreme circumstances can he get any help. This clearly implies that those people who are in positions of strength and power and are supposedly concerned with his well-being are really not-O.K. Persecutors. When he is finally so sick and devastated that he comes to the authorities' attention, they become Connections: professional suppliers of needed commodities rather than the source of any real help. Even the policeman who arrests him is really a Connection. A Wino's protesting loudly when arrested should not prevent the observer from noticing that the Wino is getting his payoff at this time and is basically pleased. The arresting policeman is just an official link to the hospital or to the jail dining hall. Winos often like to play a pastime called "Ain't It Awful?," and mental-health workers will be well advised to stay aloof from it. That is not to say that mental-health workers should pretend that it isn't awful to be a Wino or that Winos are not mistreated, but that spending a lot of time in that particular pastime is nonproductive and wasteful.

The duplicity of Wino involves police and the courts, and is exemplified by the following early-morning scene, at the drunk court, in a large western city.

Wearily eyeing a score of assorted Winos awaiting sentence, the judge went through the following dialogue with Charley:

"Charley—drunk and disorderly again."
"No, your honor, I wasn't drunk, I was just . . . "
"Okay, Okay, Charley, I know. How about thirty days in the county jail?"

Charley slams his fist into his hand ("shoot"), spins around and winks and smiles at the row of waiting prisoners as he walks back to the jail door.

At the social level, it appears that Charley is being punished for breaking the law. In reality, Charley has once again managed to put a roof over his head—with the help of the judge. The judge chooses not to face his complicity and prefers to pretend that he is somehow administering justice, when, in fact, he is actually providing Charley with a secure situation for the next few weeks.

The conviction on the part of observers of alcoholism—that alcoholics are the helpless victims of a horrible, incurable disease—might seem justified to anyone who has witnessed a hard game of Wino. The very idea that such severe self-damage could be called a game brings out cries of protest from well-meaning observers. When transactional analysts claim that alcoholism is a game, they are not saying that it is not serious, tragic, dangerous, or horrible.

We are saying only that since alcoholism is a game rather than a disease, a person can choose not to play. That may sound simple, but it is not intended to sound easy.

Evidence shows that even the most severe Wino player is capable of stopping his self-destruction: the annals of A.A. are full of examples. If one believes that alcoholism is a choice rather than a disease, then one can also believe that alcoholics can change their life—for the better.

Thus, I recommend that in dealing with alcoholics, someone who wants to help should avoid expressions of pity and sympathy that are appropriate for the terminally ill and replace them with a nurturing, loving, but tough-minded understanding: that the alcoholic chooses his own destiny. Not that there aren't enormous and sometimes seemingly unsurmountable difficulties for the alcoholic, but that the way out can be found—especially with the help of a wise therapist and some of the helping institutions which are available to alcoholics.

Especially to be avoided is that indulgent smile of warm understanding often given the alcoholic just off a binge as he humorously relates his latest escapade. This smile is colloquially called the "gallows transaction," and it is an unwitting but powerful reinforcement of the alcoholic's self-destruction, equivalent to helpfully adjusting the noose around his neck. Often alcoholic workers feel that the least they can do is to have a sense of humor about the alcoholic tragedy and that a refusal even to smile is simply a matter of unfriendliness. But the refusal to smile at the alcoholic's tragedy indicates, once again, that the therapist has not resigned himself to considering the alcoholic helpless. This leaves her free to explore what is hopeful and worthy of smiles and laughter in the alcoholic's life.

Since writing *Games Alcoholics Play,* I have come across public agencies which claim to use my book as a rationale for a tough— rather than nurturing—attitude about alcoholism. I want to clarify that what I mean by "tough-minded" is not the same as just "tough." I mean that working with alcoholics requires a clear, objective perception of the facts. But this needs to be coupled with a nurturing, loving outlook toward human beings—including alcoholics—an outlook without which the worker will be simply a tough Persecutor in helper's clothing.

True help can be given the Wino, and this should take the form of alcohol-free, decent housing, healthful food, medical care, opportunities for work, social services, A.A., and, if desired, psychotherapy. All of these should be given in a game-free context, devoid of Rescues or Persecution and, of course, drinking or any other drugs. When drunk, the Wino should be given a minimum of medical care, consistent with good practice, and helping efforts should be focused on the sober alcoholic, rather than the one who is at death's door.

7

Structural and Transactional Analysis *

Transactional Analysis, Eric Berne's theory of personality and therapy may, by now, be familiar to the reader. There have certainly been enough books on the subject sold in recent years to make a deep and lasting impact on the general public.

This short chapter provides a brief summary of the major Transactional Analysis concepts not covered in the rest of the book. If you think you know basic Transactional Analysis, you can skip this chapter. If you are not sure, you can skim it; I have italicized each new concept for easy spotting. If Transactional Analysis is new to you, it will be worth your while to read the next pages carefully.

Ego States

"Each of us is really three people." This means that people are able to act in three different ways: in their *Parents,* their *Adult,* and their *Child.* These three behavior modes are called *ego states* and are diagrammed in Figure 2.

The Child: Everyone knows that we sometimes act like children., When we are in the Child ego state, we aren't just putting on an act—we are really *being* children. We think, feel, see, and react

---

*This chapter is taken from the pamphlet *TA Made Simple.*[1] For a more thorough coverage of the topic read Berne himself in *Transactional Analysis in Psychotherapy,*[2] *Games People Play,* and *Beyond Games and Scripts.*[3]

Figure 2 The Three Ego States

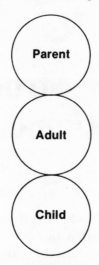

as a child. We are three or five or eight years old, and only our muscles and bones are those of a grown-up. The same is true for the Parent and Adult which are truly felt states of being, not just roles. When the Child is hateful or loving, impulsive, spontaneous, or playful, it is called the *Natural Child, Princess,* or *Prince.* When it is creative or imaginative, it is called the *Intuitive Child—*or *Little Professor.* When it is fearful, guilty or ashamed, it is called the *Adapted Child—*or *Frog.* The Child feels joy, despair, and anger— the three most basic emotions. The Child is often accused of being the source of trouble because it is self-centered, powerful, and resists being suppressed.

In TA, however, the Child is seen as the source from which the best in human beings comes: the only possible source for creativity, recreation, and procreation; the only source of renewal in life. The Child can be observed in children for extended periods of time, but also in grown-ups in situations where people have permission to let the Child out—like football games or parties. The Child will appear for short periods of time in other situations, such as board meetings, classrooms, or serious discussions, where it may not be desired at all. In its most undesirable form, it completely dominates a person's life, as in the cases of persons who are severely emotionally disturbed, like alcholics whose Child will drive them to virtual self-destruction through drinking. The Child may also appear for long periods of time in the form of depression, as in the case of people who have incurred a great loss.

For example, at Joe's Inn, Bill Winnerton, in his Child after a couple of drinks, steps into the center of the floor with Sunny Kutlo and begins to dance. His bodily gestures and language are those of a boy of eight; he moves expansively, his arms and legs swing wildly while he sings out loud. He uses words like "Wow! Far out! His experiences are those of an eight-year old as well. He not only talks and acts like a boy, but he feels like one too, which, it might be pointed out, is quite different from the way a person feels when in his Adult or Parent ego state.

The Parent: The Parent is like a tape recorder. It is a collection of prerecorded rules for living. When a person is in her Parent ego state she thinks, feels, and behaves like one of her parents or someone who took their place. The Parent decides without reasoning how to react to situations, what is good or bad, and how people should live. The Parent can be overcontrolling and oppressive, or life-giving, supportive, and tender.

One ego state can dominate a person to the exclusion of the other two. An example of this is that of the excluding Parent, which is when a person is unable to use their Child or Adult. This person is at a great disadvantage because in order to be a well-functioning human being, all the ego states must be available when needed.

An *excluding* or *fixated* Parent might be Mr. Peake, an alcoholic: "I haven't had a drink in ten years, but I feel terrible. I can't have fun. People avoid me and tell me I am boring and stuffy. I do the best I can, but I don't seem to be able to make friends. Everything seems to be okay, but I'm not happy."

Mr. Peake has to live without the benefit of his Child or Adult and is therefore cut off from two-thirds of his human potential.

The Parent can be divided into the *Nurturing Parent* and the *Critical Parent*. When the Parent is unconditionally supportive and loving, it is called the Nurturing Parent.

When the Critical Parent is overly controlling and oppressive, it is called the *Enemy Parent*. The Nurturing Parent is the Ally of the Natural Child against the Enemy.

The Parent is often used to solve problems, but it must be remembered that it bases its decisions on tradition, so it is at least 25 years behind the times—it may be as much as 250 or 2,500 years behind the times.

The Parent is useful when having to make decisions about which there is no information to be computed by the Adult, or no time to use the Adult to think; but its greatest use is the nurturing healing aspect of the person which is its natural function. The Critical Parent controls others and tries power plays. Most people with humanistic and democratic convictions shun its use altogether. When the Child is used for problem solving, it will create novel solutions based on intuition; but these solutions may not be as reliable as the fact-based Adult decisions.

The Adult: The Adult is a human biocomputer. It operates on data fed into it which it stores and uses to make computations according to a logical computing program. For instance, back at the Inn, Bill Winnerton's Adult figures out how many drinks he can buy and still have money for the turnpike tolls.

The Adult has no emotions of its own. People who think that the Adult is supposed to be the best ego state may conclude that emotions are not good. But it means only that in order to operate logically, we need to be able to keep our emotions submerged. This

Figure 3 Delusions and Contaminations

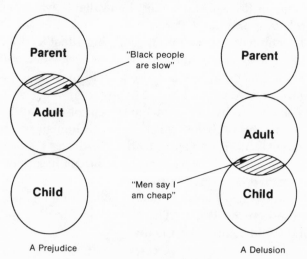

does not mean that emotions are ignored—in fact, they are important data when solving problems. It only means that emotions do not enter into the logical program of our biocomputer. When they do, the answers lose their objectivity.

This doesn't mean that being logical is the best way to be at all times. In fact, just as Mr. Peake's excluding Parent makes him an incomplete human being, so does an excluding Adult have the same deadening effect on people. People also say, "I am an adult and I have emotions!" And they are right. Being a mature human being or grown-up is not the same as being in the Adult ego state. Little children can be in their Adults, and happy grown-ups use their Parent and Child a lot.

The Adult computes all the facts fed into it. If the facts are up-to-date, then the Adult's answers will be timely and superior to the Parent's solution. If the facts are incorrect, the adult computer will produce incorrect answers. Sometimes the Adult stores data which has its source in the Child or in the Parent and which may be incorrect. This is known as *contamination*. When contamination comes from the Parent, it is called a *prejudice*. For instance, Dr. Needlepoint is a nuclear physicist who is looking for a lab assistant who can do very exacting, painstaking work with valuable equipment. In reviewing his applicants, he automatically disqualifies blacks because he believes black people are innately emotional and slow-moving, skillful with their whole bodies rather than with their hands. This data comes to Dr. Needlepoint's Adult from his Parent, and is a contamination because he has accepted it as a fact without checking it against reality.

The same unchecked acceptance of data can occur with information fed by the Child, in which case it is called a *delusion*. A delusion is usually based on the Child's fear or hope. For example, Sunny Kutlo was afraid of men. She was often sure they called her "cheap" behind her back. She *decontaminated* her Adult by checking why men looked at her and found that men looked at her because she was very beautiful, rather than cheap-looking.

Time Structure

There are five ways people can structure their time to get *strokes*.

1. A *ritual* is a preset exchange of recognition strokes. This is a four-stroke ritual:
    1. "Hi!"
    2. "How are you?"
    3. "Fine, thanks."
    4. "Well, see you around. 'Bye!"

2. A *pastime* is a preset conversation around a certain subject. Pastimes are most evident at cocktail parties and family get-togethers. Some common pastimes are "PTA" (What's Wrong with Education), "General Motors" (I like Ford, Chevy, Dodge [check one]), "Drugs" (Should Marijuana Be Legalized?), "Who's Divorcing Whom?" (Musical Beds), or "I Drink (scotch, gin, tequila) because it doesn't (give me a hangover, hurt my liver, give me bad breath)."

3. A *game* is a repetitive set of *transactions* with a covert motive and a payoff. Games have already been discussed and will be explored in greater detail in this chapter.

4. *Intimacy* is a direct and powerful exchange of strokes which people seldom use because the Child is generally prohibited by the Parent from giving and receiving strokes in this most direct way. Intimacy is not the same as sex, although it often occurs in sex. Sex, however, can also be a ritual, a pastime, a game, or work.

5. *Work* is an activity which has as its result a product and only secondarily results in the exchange of strokes.

Intimacy and work are the most satisfying ways of obtaining strokes. Unfortunately, intimacy is not available to most people, and work is often unsatisfying because people are made to work in isolation from each other and receive no personal recognition for what they produce. Therefore, people must resort to rituals, games, and pastimes which are safer—though far less satisfying—ways of obtaining strokes.

Transactions

Transactions occur when any person relates to any other person. In order to understand how people relate—transact—it is important to remember that any one person can relate from three ego states. Transactions can proceed from the Parent, Adult, or Child of one person to the Parent, Adult, or Child of another person.

The transactions in the following three examples are called parallel because they go back and forth between two ego states.

Figure 4A: Here we see a parallel transaction between Adult and Adult. Every Transaction is made up of a *stimulus* and *response.*

Stimulus: "Did you buy beer today?"

And the response is: "Yes, two six-packs."

The stimulus in a parallel Parent to Child transaction (Figure 4B) might be:

"Did you spend all the money on beer?"

And the response might be: "Yes, and it's none of your business, either!"

The following is another parallel transaction—this time, Parent to Parent (Figure 4C):

"Bill spends a lot of his money on booze. He'll never straighten out."

"I know. Alcoholics have no respect for anything. They're hopeless."

Parallel transactions don't need to be pleasant or friendly; they need only proceed smoothly between two ego states.

Sometimes transactions will involve three or four ego states, in which case they are crossed. In a *crossed transaction* the transactional response is addressed to an ego state different from the one which started the stimulus.

For example, Figure 5:

"Did you buy beer today?"

"Yes. Why don't you get off my back?"

Here the question was from Mrs. Winnerton's Adult to Billy's Adult, and the answer was from Billy's Child to Mrs. Winnerton's Parent. This is a crossed transaction; crossed transactions are important because they disrupt communication. Smooth communication can continue between ego states as long as transactions are parallel, even if their content is unpleasant or unfriendly. This is true of all parallel transactions: Adult to Adult, Parent to Adult, Parent to Parent, Child to Child, and so forth. This is useful to know because it can be used to figure out, in a string of transac-

Figure 4

Figure 4A Adult to Adult Parallel Transaction

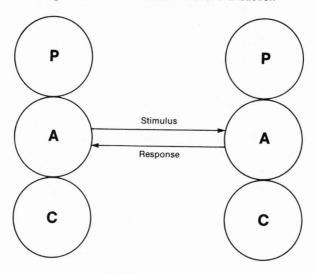

Bill: "Did you buy beer?"
Natalie: "Yes, two six-packs."

Figure 4B Parent to Child Parallel Transaction

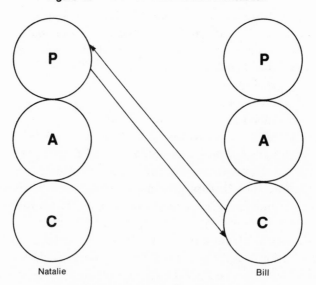

Stimulus: "Did you spend all the money?"
Response: "None of your business!"

Figure 4C   Parent to Parent Parallel Transaction

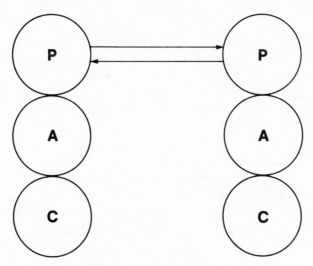

"Bill will never straighten out."
"I know, alcoholics have no respect."

Figure 5   A Crossed Transaction

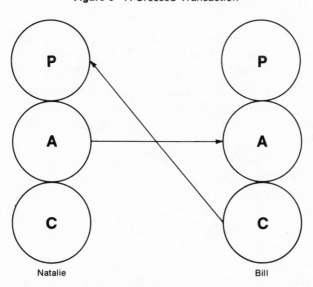

Natalie: "Did you buy beer?"
Bill: "Get off my back!"

tions, precisely where communication was disrupted. The rule is: Whenever a disruption of communication occurs, a crossed transaction caused it.

One very important kind of crossed transaction is the *discount* transaction. Here, one person completely disregards what the other one is saying. Discounts are not always obvious, but are always unpleasant to the person receiving them, and if repeated can make people quite upset and eventually make them feel crazy. For example:

Bill: "I'm afraid and can't sleep. I need a drink."

Natalie: "Don't be silly. There is nothing to be afraid of. Just go to sleep. You don't need a drink."

Here Natalie is ignoring Bill's worry about sleeping and tries to get him to forget it. Her move probably won't work.

Covert Transactions

A *covert* transaction occurs when people say one thing and mean another. Covert transactions are the basis of games and are especially interesting because they are crooked. They have a *social* (overt) and a *psychological* (covert) level. Example (Figure 6):
Social Level:
Boss: Let's work late, Miss Phistie, and I'll buy you dinner.

Secretary: That's a good idea; there is a lot of work to do.
Covert Level:
Bill: I love your smile, Natalie. Let's have dinner and drinks and really get to know each other.

Natalie: I thought you would never ask, Bill. I've wanted to go out with you for quite a while.

It is important to know the difference between the social and covert levels, because in order to understand and predict what people are going to do, the social level is generally useless. Based on the social level of this transaction, Mrs. Winnerton would expect to reach Bill Winnerton at the office in the evenings. If Mrs. Winnerton were aware of the psychological level of the relationship, she'd know to call Joe's Inn.

We say one thing and mean another because we are generally ashamed of our Child's wishes and desires. Nevertheless, we act on

Figure 6 A Covert Transaction

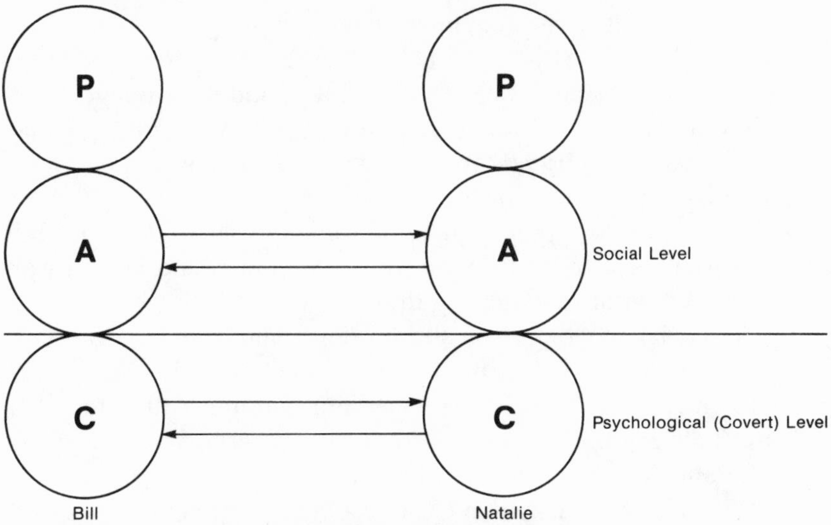

Social Level
Boss: "Let's work late."
Secretary: "Good idea."

Covert Level
Bill: "Let's have dinner and drinks."
Natalie: "Goody, a party!"

these desires while we pretend to be doing otherwise. For instance, we may use smiling sarcasm instead of a direct expression of our anger. When we are scared, we may counterattack instead of admitting our fears.

When we want strokes, we often feign indifference—and we have trouble giving strokes to people when we want to. In fact, because lying is so prevalent between people and by politicians and advertisers, our lives are immersed in half truth and deception so that we no longer clearly know how we feel and what we really want. We also don't expect people to be completely honest so that we never really know whether we can trust them.

Games

Now that we know what a covert transaction is, we can talk about games because one basic aspect of games is their crookedness or covertness. In fact, a game is a recurring series of ulterior transactions with a beginning, middle, and end, and a payoff.

Let's look at a very common game people play: "Why Don't You, Yes But" (YDYB). "Why Don't You, Yes But" is a good example of a game's definite beginning and end, and its two levels.

Seven years after Natalie Phistie and Bill Winnerton got married, she and some friends are having a discussion over coffee while her husband is out bowling:

Natalie: I'm so upset—I just don't know what to do about Bill. He doesn't seem to be listening to me anymore, and he is always running out on me and getting drunk.

Friend 1: Why don't you sit him down and have a serious talk?

Natalie: Yes, I've tried that, but he won't sit still.

Friend 2: You probably are spending too much time together. Why don't you take a vacation from each other?

Natalie: Yes, but we can't afford it.

Friend 3: Well, why don't you just get a divorce?

Natalie: Yes, but what about the kids?

Friends (each thinking): I give up—this situation is hopeless . . .

Natalie (thinking): Nobody loves me.

Obviously, this conversation is recurring. Natalie has been through it many times; her friends have been through it many times. As a matter of fact, much of their time has been spent playing "Why Don't You, Yes But," and it is the type of conversation which occurs over and over again, especially in therapy groups. It is crooked and covert: on the social level, it appears to be a conversation between a person in her Adult ego state asking questions of a group of others who are also in their Adult ego states.

However, notice that Natalie does not accept any of the group's suggestions. The reason: at the psychological and much more meaningful level, Natalie is really, deviously asking for strokes. But she needs a great many strokes and therefore must continue to ask for them.

Further, because these strokes are being given deviously, they are not as satisfying to either Natalie or her friends as direct strokes would be. This is why the game ends on a note of frustration. The payoff of this game is that it proves to Natalie that she is not lovable, just as her father said; and it proves to her friends that there is no use trying to help friends because they never accept advice anyway.

A better understanding of the payoff game can be gained from examining another common game, "Rapo":

While Natalie is talking to her friends, Bill is not at the bowling alley—but at Joe's Inn. He is sitting next to Sunny Kutlo. They are flirting. He buys her a drink, and she lights his cigarette. He touches her arm, and she touches his knee. Meanwhile they are in a deep conversation about history. They decide to visit the old oak tree where General Custer rested on the way to his last stand. Sitting in Bill's convertible in the moonlight while listening to "Come on, Baby, Light My Fire," Bill makes a sexual advance but Sunny does not have sex on her mind. She leaps out of the car angrily, leaving Bill dumbfounded. Bill is the Victim in Rapo, and Sunny is the Persecutor.

They have both played this game before; in every case, what appeared to be a Child-to-Child flirtation at the social level was at the covert level first a come-on and then a putdown. In this case, Bill was the Victim; but he also plays the game as Persecutor. He does this by encouraging women to love him and then, when they do, accusing them of clinging. He then abruptly "Rapo"s them by terminating the relationship. With his wife, he plays "Rapo" as the Persecutor when she asks, "Do you love me?" and he answers, "Sure, I love you—quit bugging me."

Payoffs

Why do Bill and Sunny play this game? Every game pays off for the players at three different levels:

1. The *biological payoff* of a game is strokes.

Even though the game ended badly, both Bill and Sunny got a considerable number of strokes—both positive and negative—out of it.

2. The *social payoff* of a game is time-structuring.

Both Bill and Sunny filled a whole evening, which otherwise might have been very dull, with an exciting activity.

3. The *existential* payoff of a game is the way in which the game confirms the *existential position* of each player.

Let's explain what existential position is all about. Every person defines for himself early in life what the meaning of his life or existence is. Some people decide they are O.K. and are going to have a good life; many others decide they are not O.K. and will fail.

For example, Sunny was told by her father that men are no good, and by implication that she would never meet a man who could love her. Because Sunny believed her father, the game of "Rapo" confirms his prediction about her life. When she walks away from Bill, she affirms in her own mind that, just like Daddy said, men are creeps and no one will truly love her. This is her existential position. Games are always played with equal responsibility and interest by all the players. Bill's part in the game with Sunny is just as important as hers, and he derives a payoff from it as well.

Bill and his mother had a relationship in which she often distrusted him and was after him, which made him feel not O.K. And he often heard his father say, "Women will get the upper hand on you, any way they can. Watch out, son."

Bill decided he would indeed watch out. When he chooses Sunny at the bar for a partner, he knows the evening will end in failure. What he wants is strokes, but he believes that either she will turn him down or that he will eventually have to turn her down. If he likes her, he will expect "Rapo"; if she likes him, he will have to watch out because she is sure to have expectations which will eventually become nagging demands. Either way, he never risks a disruption of his plan, which calls for failure with women. His existential payoff in the game of "Rapo" is the confirmation of the validity of his decision that he would never succeed with a woman. This decision is part of a *script* of loneliness and lovelessness which governs Bill's life.

8

Alcoholism and Scripts

In previous chapters, I have attempted to show that alcoholism is a game. But, in addition to being an addiction, a bad habit and a game, alcoholism is also a script.

A script is a life plan. It isn't unusual for people to make decisions about how they are going to live their lives and then stick by them. Young people decide to be firefighters, nurses, engineers, lawyers, and police officers, and then stick to that decision. People also decide to get married or not to get married, to have no, one, two, or more children, to work hard or to be depressed, to commit suicide or to be alcoholic. Every one of these decisions becomes part of a life plan.

So the script is a life plan. But it isn't just any life plan, it is a life plan which is rigid and unchangeable. Like the lines of a play, a life plan expects to be followed word by word from beginning to end and allows for very little improvisation. A script is written by somebody else, and like actors who may initially have a choice to participate or not, once we have signed up for a particular play we feel bound by ourselves and others to act the part to the bitter or happy ending.

Precisely as in a play, the script can be a drama, or a melodrama, it can have a good or bad ending, and this will determine whether the audience leaves the theater smiling or with tears in their eyes. Depending on whether we put on a good or bad performance, the play will be forgotten as soon as it is over or it will be remembered for a few hours, a day, a lifetime, or generations. Regardless of the audience's reaction, however, a script is still written by someone else; and whether we read its lines lamely or convincingly, we feel compelled to stay, to continue, to finish. We can't think of anything to do other than to remain in the security of the stage and repeat our well-worn lines even as we realize that we don't want to be there and that we are wasting our lives.

The striking similarities between dramatic scripts and our lives were observed by Eric Berne, who incorporated the analysis of people's life scripts into his early writings on Transactional Analysis. Since Berne's introduction of the concept of scripts into psychiatry much has been done to discover how scripts become a part of our lives. A great deal has been written since Berne's early writings, some of it by myself; some of it, later, by Berne; and some of it by others in Transactional Analysis. Much attention has been paid to how scripts are transmitted and by whom, how they are kept alive, what kinds of scripts there are, and how people can release themselves from them.

After many years of work with scripts, my own interest has narrowed to how we can give them up, rather than how we get them. Who wrote the script, why we decided to be players in it, and even what the script is called, are not nearly as interesting to me now as how I can help myself and others to look up from our tightly held libretto and, as the audience watches in astonishment, turn on our heels and, ignoring the protests of other players, directors, and producers, walk into the backstage alley leaving the show behind as we search for a genuine, autonomous, and spontaneous way of life.

Specifically, the script of alcoholism, which we are all so familiar with, can be given up as well. The alcoholic can decide to stop reading his well-worn lines and move, instead, to change his life. Because my interest has become focused on how to *give up* the script, this book will deal with script analysis very differently than my previous books and will reveal in more detail the way I practice script analysis rather than the theories I hold about it.

People Are Born O.K.

Children are born with an innate potential for spontaneity, awareness, and intimacy—or, as Eric Berne put it, "People are born princes and princesses." Depending on what kind of a household or situations they are delivered into by fate, their development from princehood into their full potential may be fully allowed, may be nipped in the bud, or may be permitted to muddle along. If we looked realistically at the thousands of children who are born every day, we would see that only a few lucky ones will be given true freedom to choose. Many face starvation from the first day on, many will never have even the basic human right to speak freely or to express their emotions—let alone to choose for or against in matters of importance to their lives.

We in North America have an unusual range of choices and reasonable freedom to choose between them, especially if we are white middle-class Americans. Even so, approximately 10 percent of us will become slaves to alcohol. One-fourth of us will be addicted to cigarettes and (this is my guess) as many as one-half will find ourselves dominated by some form of addiction: caffeine, sugar, fattening foods, prescription or over-the-counter drugs, alcohol, or narcotics.

Personal Responsibility

How does it happen that in spite of having the capacity for choosing any kind of life, we wind up with the particular enslaving scripts that we live?

Lately, a monumental piece of nonsense has reached almost complete acceptance in the minds of people devoted to pop psychology. It is the notion of "personal responsibility." According to this point of view, people are completely responsible for their experiences in life. People choose what they do, and if their lives aren't working satisfactorily, they can choose to be poor, and people who are rich choose to be rich. People who are not loved have a need not to be loved and could find a faithful lover merely by wishing it. People who are ill can choose health; people who are persecuted can choose to be free.

According to this view, we have no one but ourselves to blame for the quandaries in which we find ourselves; life is exactly as we want it to be and if we wanted it to be otherwise we could simply change it. There is no point in blaming our parents or teachers, our government or the media, the oil companies or General Motors for the quality of our lives; we are free to choose whether we want to be happy or unhappy, employed or unemployed, healthy or sick. Those holding this view, which can be called the "idiotic theory," remind me of the finger who, because it could move this way and that, every time it wanted to, developed the delusion that it was separate from the other fingers and in complete charge of its own destiny. The Greek word *idiotes* means separate individual. Hence this little finger's delusion can be justly called idiotic.[1] It is plain to the observer that the finger is attached to a hand and that its everyday life and destiny is intimately tied to factors beyond its control.

The absurd notion of total personal responsibility has been successfully sold to people through millions of copies of best-selling books such as *Pulling Your Own Strings* by Wayne W. Dyer,[2] *Success!* by Michael Korda,[3] and *Looking Out for No. 1* by Robert Ringer,[4] etc. In addition, est and other human potential movement ideologies espouse this view which has by now become an absolute dogma within the movement.

I won't go into why their view has gained such universal acceptance. I do want to make sure that you don't mistakenly conclude that this is yet another book proposing that we are completely responsible for whatever happens to us; that alcoholism is simply a self-chosen path on which a person can easily decide to drink, to be sober, or to drink socially.

Let us, however, look further into this notion and ask ourselves why the myth of personal responsibility is so appealing to people. The idea does have a substantial grain of truth; we do choose just how we are going to live our lives. However, the choices we have to begin with are less than overwhelmingly varied. We have approximately as wide a choice of life-styles as we have of presidential candidates. We are free to select between Tweedledee and Tweedledum. Whether we choose between one crooked path or politician or another, the freedom that we have is very relative.

Of course, we may choose to be unhappily married, but what are our alternatives? On a job application, we are allowed to pick between being single, married, divorced, or widowed. Lately a goodly number of us are choosing none of the above and simply living with the one we love. O.K., so add "living together" to S, M,

D, or W. How many of us have any "legitimate" choices beyond those? How about "In love with one person, living with another"? or "Married to two other women"? or "Living with mother"? or "Celibate"?

Sure, we choose to drop out of high school or to stay in and go to to college, but how many of us can choose (realistically now) to drop out of high school *and then* go to college—unless we have well-to-do parents?

Sure, we decide to drink coffee and booze, eat doughnuts and get fat and develop back trouble. But how many of us can work eight hours and commute two hours a day, cook, do the dishes, take care of the kids and the dog and then jog for an hour, when the streets aren't safe after 6 P.M.? Sure, we choose to drink, drink, drink from noon to bedtime, but we are also addicted and don't know it. We are pressured to drink by friends, coworkers, and employers, and we aren't allowed any other avenue for the expression of our needs, or for fun, love, and human contact.

Also, in addition to being very narrow, most choices are made in the distant past, and they have consequences not so easily changed as the myth suggests. It is as if life was a walk through a thick forest. If, early in the day we choose a certain fork on the path and decide by noontime that we made a mistake, the right path can be found—but not all that simply.

So, yes, we choose, but we choose among the alternatives available to us at the time, and we choose before we know much about what our choice means or leads to. That can hardly be translated into the claim that we are fully responsible for the shape our lives take.

Another reason that people cling to the view of total responsibility is because it gives them a feeling of power over their lives. "If I didn't believe that I have power over my life, I could become completely discouraged, I'd want to give up and kill myself," a friend once told me. Psychotherapists who espouse the idiotic view seem to be convinced that anything short of taking complete responsibility would cause their "patients" to give up all efforts to change and settle into a mire of irresponsible blaming.

My experience with this matter is different. I believe that people's lives are the result of a combination of external and internal factors. An alcoholic is an alcoholic because her father was an alcoholic and because she decided to sneak drinks when she was a teenager. She is surrounded by people and advertising which encourage her to drink, and she chooses to associate with those people, instead of going to A.A. meetings. She is overworked and exhausted from an ill-paying and monotonous job and she doesn't eat or sleep properly when she is off work. Her choices are combined with external influences to shape her life. It is a fifty-fifty proposition.

When I explain this to people, they don't respond by giving up and blaming the world for their problems. They simply come to see more clearly why their lives are what they are and why, at times, they feel powerless over them. So far as I can see, this realization only leads to renewed efforts and power rather than to giving up.

Powerlessness

One experience is common to all addictions, and that is the feeling of powerlessness. Being unable to control one's behavior is an experience which tends to occupy a large portion of a person's consciousness and at times completely overwhelms it. Not having the power to stop the use of cigarettes, sleeping pills, coffee, alcohol, amphetamines, heroin, or marijuana, when we know they are harmful, is most damaging to self-esteem. When we experience the humiliation of powerlessness, it poisons our life, makes us feel worthless, contemptible, and ashamed. We look around and see other people who appear to be in control of their lives, doing what they must do, avoiding what they must not. Yet we see ourselves chained to our habits, powerless to control our own actions.

Many people manage to avoid confronting their powerlessness by telling themselves and others that the amount of coffee or cigarettes or alcohol they consume is reasonable, that there is no problem, that they are in fact consuming these substances they abuse because they want to and because they enjoy it, and don't see anything wrong with it. There are millions of people who smoke a couple of packs of cigarettes, drink five or six cups of coffee, and consume four or five ounces of alcohol every day, and claim that this is just as they would like it to be. When we recognize such a situation in ourselves or in others, it is important not to make any moral judgments. My point here is not that five cups of coffee, two packs of cigarettes, or five ounces of alcohol a day are a problem, even though I believe they are. What I am saying is that I don't believe there are many people who would disagree that tranquilizers, coffee, cigarettes, or alcohol are not good for you. When people find themselves abusing them, they secretly would like to stop.

What people really think about drinking, smoking, and drinking coffee is clearly revealed by how they react when their children start to do so. John Q. Public may claim that his habits are no problem, but what will his reaction be when his twelve-year-old child starts to drink coffee, smoke cigarettes, and drink just as he does? The response is usually quite passionate and reveals what the person truly feels about the matter.

The terror that comes with the realization of how hooked we really are is one of the greatest obstacles to people's success in kicking their habits. I know of no one who enjoys being hooked, but discovering that you are powerless to stop doing things you don't want to do is an experience people wish to avoid. Consequently, many who know and believe that it would be desirable to do something about their habits simply do not attempt it because they believe they will fail, and, quite understandably, do not want to face the humiliation of their impotence.

One of the factors that contributes to people's fear of tackling their addictions is the myth of personal power mentioned above. Many people have the idea that "anyone who really wants to stop can just go ahead and do it," and that "if you really want to stop, you can," and that, in fact, "you can do anything you want to." The facts of life are that there is more to getting what we want than meets the eye, and when we try and try, meeting only with failure or partial success while everyone else seems to be getting what they want, we are liable to feel that there is something drastically wrong with us. We blame ourselves for our failures and we feel powerless. The facts of addictions, and the grip they have on our bodies, are sobering. It isn't just a simple matter of stopping. We may need help. But we are brought up to believe that anybody who is anybody can do whatever he needs to do by himself, without any help. To need help is to show weakness; to admit to powerlessness is humiliating and frowned upon. To seek advice, to request nurturing, are taboo. This is especially true for men in our culture, who are told that doing it alone, without help, without discussion, is how it really should be done. The same attitude affects women as well, though to a lesser degree.

It is true that some people do it alone. But the majority of people can greatly profit from understanding that their habits are very powerful, that help is needed, and that doing it alone is unnecessary, foolish, and prideful, while doing it with other people's help is intelligent, human, and effective.

There is a childhood prank which we used to play on people in the streets of Mexico City. We stuck a long piece of iron bar in the ground so that only a short piece protruded and then put a can over it. People would come up to the can, instinctively kick it, and find, to their amazement and sometimes pain, that the can was stuck in place. The way in which some people attempt to deal with their addictions reminds me of this prank. Some people approach their addictions with supreme confidence, thinking that to kick them would be as easy as to kick an empty can down the street, only to find that there is a great deal more to the kicking than they had anticipated.

By ignoring the realities of addiction and blaming ourselves for lacking "willpower," we make ourselves more powerless than we really are. It is not necessary to become humiliated in the process of kicking our habits: addictions are difficult to kick. With help it can be done, but almost never easily.

Parental Influences

If we aren't totally responsible for the choices in our lives, who is? A major determinant of the choices we have and make as children is who our parents were and how they behaved toward us. If our parents love and are glad to have us, make room for us, feed and cuddle us, pay attention to us and protect us from harm, trust us, give us permission to explore the world and do not have any rigid, preconceived ideas of what we must or must not do, then our choices will be many and varied. But if our parents had us by accident, are not glad to see us come into the world, have no room for us, ignore us, resent us, mistrust us, and are afraid for us, then they'll want to channel our lives into narrow, preconceived paths and will give us few choices. Why we treat our children the way we do is related to our own circumstances. A woman whose husband is an alcoholic may not want another child—least of all a boy. She may resent him and punish him for fear that he will grow to be mean and irresponsible like his father. Or she may love the boy and want to protect him from the world's lessons by keeping him isolated and fearing his every independent move.

I would like to put aside, for a minute, the social conditions into which we are born and which directly affect us and our parents. I would like to focus, instead, on two essential aspects of our parent's personalities, which have much to do with our choice of scripts.

The Parent ego state is an externally acquired replica of another person which is incorporated and becomes a major part of us. In addition to the Parent ego state, each person also has an Adult ego state and a Child ego state. All three of these ego states— Parent, Adult, and Child in our parents—are to us, as little children, our mother or father. If our parents relate to us mostly from a nurturing, loving, accepting, protecting, Parent ego state, then we will see our mother or father as being loving, nurturing, and protective, and our own Parent ego state will be a loving, nurturing and protective ally. If our parents relate to us in an angry, demanding, impatient, controlling, careless, jealous, competitive Child ego state, then our Parent ego state will in turn be an angry, demanding, careless and competitive enemy. The Parent ego state that we learn as children will be primarily a replica of the behavior that our parents exhibited toward us when we were children.

There has been much debate in Transactional Analysis about the how, what, where and when of the causes of the script. After many years of participation in that debate, I am ready to say that to me, in my work as a therapist, very little of this debate has made any difference except the understanding of the Critical Parent and of the Nurturing Parent and how they develop.

9

The Two Parents

Sometimes in adolescence we are delivered into the cruel world with a Parent ego state which is an internalization or adaptation of the various parental influences which we were exposed to and which shows itself in one of two forms:

The Nurturing Parent or Ally: This Parent ego state holds the view that people are O.K. and need to be given free rein. It is a nurturing ego state that wants to take care of people, feed them, clothe them, shelter them, and protect them from harmful influences. It provides for the necessities of life while it encourages self-determination. When it doesn't succeed, it becomes sad and worried.

The Critical Parent or Enemy: This ego state believes that people are not O.K. and need to be controlled and shown what is right and what is wrong. It is primarily concerned with preventing people from doing certain things and manipulating them into doing certain others. It is willing to use force and all manner of power plays to achieve its purpose. When it doesn't succeed, it becomes angry and violent.

One of these two Parent ego states dominates the small family world in which we were brought up, but no family is completely devoid of the other. As we learn our daily lessons from our parents, they become part of our own personality as our own Parent ego state, and when we finally leave mother and father behind, these two Parent ego states remain inside of us to become major influences in our behavior. We will perpetuate our parental treatment of us in our treatment of our own Child ego state. Our own spontaneous, aware, and intimate selves will be treated either with nurturing or with harsh criticism by us. We will also treat others— especially those whom we see as children—with the same nurturance or harshness. In this manner we will perpetuate the influences of our childhood in ourselves, in our children, and in other people. To the extent that we do it to others, we are promoting, perpetrating, and colluding with other people's scripts. Because of this, the study of the Ally and the Enemy is essential to the understanding of scripts and of alcoholism.

Readers must not confuse the following discussion of the Nurturing and Critical Parents with a discussion of actual parents. The Ally and the Enemy are ego states which exist in everyone. We are interested in the Ally and Enemy in the parents of people because they are the main influence in scripting. In addition, the Critical and Nurturing Parent play major roles in people's lives.

Eric Berne said, "People are born princes and princesses until their parents turn them into frogs." It is as if the newborn child is faced not just with father and mother, but with a complicated cast of characters made up of all their ego states plus all the ego states of brothers and sisters, cousins, aunts, and grandparents. There will be fun-loving, sad, or creative children and studious or intuitive Adults; but there will also be loving, protective fairy godmothers and fathers and wicked, abusive ogres and witches. Just as in childhood fairy tales, these characters are of major importance in our early lives and remain important throughout our lives.

When and if they enter our lives, these real-life witches and ogres lay various "curses" on us. They tell us what we are going to do and what is going to happen to us. They prohibit us from thinking so that we must drink to solve our problems, or they disallow our feelings so that we carry them around bottled up, waiting for an excuse to to pull the cork and let them go. They prohibit us from acting, threatening punishment of eternal sleep or being turned into frogs or ugly ducklings. In short, they frighten us into giving up our birthright of aliveness and settle for an approved life path in which choices are made *for* us rather than *by* us.

Many people try to rebel against this tyranny. Some of us, with the help of fairy godmothers, succeed in escaping the curse. But most of us choose to give in and become comfortable frogs. We wait until we leave the ancestral home to find the one who will give us the magic kisses that will turn us back into our original princely shape.

Let us look at these two protagonists—the Nurturing Parent or Ally and the Critical Parent or Enemy—and how they affect our lives as we travel the path between birth and death.

An Afternoon at the Supermarket

There is an easily available place to observe Nurturing and Critical Parents; a supermarket on a busy Friday afternoon. Tired by a hard day's work, dazed by the rows and rows of hypnotically designed packages, mothers and fathers cart their children through the aisles as they try to get the next week's shopping done. The children want candy, cookies, potato chips, and soda pop. They want to be carried, or they want to push the cart, or they want to ride in it and throw its contents back onto the shelves. They ask questions, beg to be held, giggle, cry, interrupt, get lost, break jars of mayonnaise or honey, as they exercise their drive toward spontaneity, awareness, and intimacy. Regardless of how exhausted they are, we can still clearly see two patterns of Parent behavior: nurturance and harshness, sometimes exclusive of each other, sometimes following one another in rapid sequence, sometimes bursting out in furtive excesses of anger or love.

One mother, alone with a one-year-old and a four-year-old speed demon is trying to decide whether it will be Purox or Clorex this time while the older boy tugs at her pant leg and shakes a box of animal crackers against her thigh. The little one sitting in the cart is drooling all over her purse as he sucks on a overripe peach which mother reluctantly let him have after she gave in to his insistent whining.

"Stop it!" she begs while she tries to compare prices and contents. "Stop it, I said." The anklebiter is undaunted. She squats down. "Pleeeese, would you stop it? What do you want? Can't you see I'm trying to shop?" There is strain and desperation in her voice. Yet her free hand cradles his head gently and her anger is not really directed at him. He starts crying.

The peach splats on the linoleum next to them. Anger flashes in mother's eyes as she straightens up. The little one is startled and frightened; mother's tight-lipped anger melts as she wipes his face and gives him a kiss. "You nut," she says, "I'm going to flip out. Let's get out of here."

"Cut!"

A woman enters from the sidelines. "That was good—I think we can use it. Let's try the Enemy now—take it from the top." She disappears. We are back to the beginning of the scene.

"Stop it!" This time the mother's voice is harsh. Her leg pushes the child away as her hand slaps his and almost knocks the crackers out of it. She squats down and grabs his arm, shaking him. "Can't you see I'm trying to shop? What do you want?" She pushes him away. "Take those back where you got them. And don't you start crying!" She hits him on the butt with her open hand, propelling him away from her.

Splat! She bolts up. "No! No! No!!!" She furiously tears up a package of paper towels and, with teeth clenched, roughly wipes the little one's face and then the floor. Her face stony, she wheels the cart away. There is an ominous feeling left behind as she turns into the next aisle and the cries of the children fade into the background din of the the shoppers.

The Enemy and the Ally

Let us look at several other situations in which the contrast between the Enemy and the Ally can be more easily seen. (The dialogues are annotated for future reference.)

Tommy's grades have arrived throught the mail and the family is having dinner around the table. Father has had a couple of drinks.

Father (bitterly): Well, Tom, it looks like you are not going to make it to college. (1)

Tommy (surprised): What do you mean?

Father reaches into his pocket and pulls out the report card:

Look at these. What are you trying to do? Are you trying to get an award for the lowest grades in history? (2)

Tommy: Let me see that.

Father hands him the grades.

Tommy: That bitch, Mrs. Spruce—she's picking on me again. I worked real hard on that essay, and she still gave me an F.

Father: Don't swear at the goddamn table and don't try to blame it on the teacher. I haven't seen you do any homework for weeks. All I can tell you is this: if you aren't even going to graduate from high school, (3) you had better start looking for a job real quick. (4) I'm not supporting a bum (5) around this house.

Tommy: I don't need you to support me. I'll get a job—don't worry.

Father: Sure, lots of luck. (6) Let's hope that you keep it longer than you kept your summer job. That lasted exactly a week. You'd better get going on something around here, or there is going to be hell to pay.

In the above exchange, Tommy's father was acting as the Enemy. Let us see how the Ally would handle the situation.

Father (worried): Tom, I want to talk to you. (1) (He pulls the report card out of his pocket and lays it in front of the boy.) I just got this in the mail and it doesn't look too good. What's going on, Tommy? (2)

Tommy (picks up the card and looks at it intently): "That bitch, Mrs. Spruce—she's picking on me. I worked real hard on that essay, and she still gave me an F.

Father. There's no point in blaming the teacher for this. What happened? Why are your grades so low? (3)

Tommy: Well, I'm trying to study, Dad. I just don't seem to be getting anywhere. I put a lot of work into that essay, and it still wasn't good enough.

Father: Well, I haven't seen you do any homework in the last month. Maybe you're working hard, but perhaps you're not working hard enough. Or maybe you need some help. (4) You had better do something, though, because it looks to me like you are not going to be able to finish high school and I'm worried (5) that you won't be able to find a job the way things are nowadays.

Tommy: Don't worry, I'll find a job.

Father: Well, I *am* worried, and I think it is important that you take this school business a little more seriously because things are rough out there, and they are even rougher for people who don't finish high school. Maybe I can help you with your homework.

Tommy: Sure. When you come home from work, you are too tired and you want to read the paper or watch TV. You never listen to what I tell you; you wouldn't be able to help me with my homework.

Father: I know what you're saying is true, and I know it is a problem, (6) but I think we had better get on this before things get really bad and you do flunk out of high school. Let's give it a try.

Contrasting these two examples, we see how Tommy's father, in the Enemy role, attributes failure and scares Tommy by suddenly bringing up the topic of his grades (1). Next he ridicules (2) and soon again attributes failure (3), threatens (4), and insults (5) Tommy. This is followed by sarcasm (6) and renewed threats.

In the Ally role, Tommy's father avoids threats, insults, and sarcasm. He avoids scaring Tommy, and he does not attribute failure to him. Instead, he brings up the subject carefully and gently, (1) he asks questions (2), (3), he suggest solutions (4), talks about his feelings (5), and accepts some responsibility for the problem (6).

Let's look at an example relating to drug abuse.

Uncle Charlie and Joan are having a conversation which he leads around to drugs.

Charlie: If there's one thing I can't stand it's seeing those kids racing around in their cars and drinking beer. It makes me sick.

Joan: Well, *you* drive and smoke marijuana; what are you complaining about?

Charlie: "That's different. Marijuana doesn't affect your driving. You can actually drive better when you are stoned. Anyway, I don't smoke it that much. Those kids probably drink and smoke and do uppers and downers all at once.

Joan: They drink because it's the only thing they can buy to get high on.

Charlie: Yeah, that's all they can think of: getting high, sex, and cars. Seems to me that when I was their age, I had better things on my mind. These kids don't seem to have any brains at all. Why do you defend them—are you drinking booze, too? Come on, don't lie to me. I know you are! You are just like all the others.

Joan: There you go again, I hate you! You always start these arguments in that sneaky way of yours. Leave me alone.

Again, let's try the nurturing approach.

Charlie: I'm really surprised to see that all the kids are going back to drinking alcohol again. I thought the young people had gotten some sense. I'm really disappointed to see all of that come back. Do you drink alcohol, Joan?

Joan: Sure I do. What do you think? It's the only thing I can get to get high.

Charlie: But don't you realize that alcohol is really harmful and that you can get addicted to it?

Joan: What am I supposed to do—smoke marijuana like you do? For one thing, it's illegal. For another, it's hard to get. For another, my friends aren't into it. So what am I supposed to do—borrow a joint from you and get stoned by myself?

Charlie: I don't know what to tell you. I just know that drinking and driving is very dangerous. I don't like the pattern that I see your friends in, and I wish you wouldn't get involved in it.

Joan: Well, I'm not all that involved in it, and I don't actually like to drive with the kids while they are drinking. We actually do smoke marijuana anyway, but there is very little I can do except to stay away from the gang, and sometimes I actually do that. Some of my girlfriends and I really don't like it at all, and we often stay away from the whole thing.

Charlie: Well, I can see that it's a problem any way you look at it. Drugs will always be a problem, I suppose. Let me know if there is anything I can do, and please take care of yourself.

Joan: Thanks. I'll keep that in mind, and I'll take care of myself.

These exaggerated examples of Critical Parent and Nurturing Parent behavior illustrate the way in which the Enemy makes categorical not-O.K. judgments of others, predicts not-O.K. outcomes, attributes not-O.K. features to people, and attempts to control behavior without a real understanding of what it is dealing with. In contrast, the Ally tries to protect children from harm, assumes people are O.K., expects O.K. outcomes, assumes that people are well intentioned and cooperative, and attempts to guide people's lives not through control but through negotiation and encouragement.

The alcoholic's Enemy typically persecutes its owner with insults ("You're drunk, weak-willed, stupid") injunctions ("Don't think," "Don't trust," "Don't feel") and attributions (Once a drunk, always a drunk. You'll never straighten out"). In the face of such harassment, the Ally will counter with strokes ("You're strong and smart"), permissions ("Think, Trust, Feel") and positive attributions ("You will change," "You can be completely O.K.").

Combined with a well-informed Adult and fun-loving, joyful Child, the Ally is a positive influence in people's lives. In contrast, the Enemy is usually combined with an inhibited, constricted Child and whether or not it is connected with a knowledgeable Adult, the combination of Enemy and Adapted Child (or frog) is conducive to the formation of scripts. Eventually the child incorporates the Critical Parent and then proceeds to deal with others and his or her own Child ego state in the same manner in which his parents taught him. Eventually the Enemy becomes the respository of all the not-O.K. messages, the prison guard that jails the Child's awareness, intimacy, and spontaneity and which prevents thinking about or making the changes which might abolish the script and redirect life in a more workable direction. What this has to do with alcoholism will be explored in depth in the next chapter.

Most fathers and mothers will use both Parental ego states at different times. The point is not that mother *was* an Ally or father *was* an Enemy, the point is that they related to their child from one or the other ego state at important times which set precedents in the child's scripting. No parent is all good or all bad, though some are extreme. Witness, for instance, the thousands of yearly cases of child abuse in this country alone. Extreme Nurturance exists, too, but does not make the headlines.

The script of joylessness tends to be found among drug abusers. It has the specific effect of making people vulnerable to addiction and social pressure to drink. Before this specific script is explored, it is necessary to the principles of radical psychiatry which will be needed to understand the chapter on joylessness.

10

Alienation and Power in the World

To understand the existence of the Enemy, it is necessary to examine the phenomenon of alienation and its opposite, power in the world.

Alienation as the source of human unhappiness has been extensively studied by Radical Psychiatry, a theory of psychotherapy and personality which originated in Berkeley in the late 1960s. What follows is a brief summary of that theory. A complete statement of the theory can be found in my book, *Readings in Radical Psychiatry*,[1] and in Hogie Wyckoff's book, *Solving Women's Problems*.[2]

Radical Psychiatry draws a number of its ideas from Eric Berne's Transactional Analysis. One principal Transactional Analysis concept is that people are O.K.; or, as we say in radical pyschiatry, they are, by their nature, capable of living in harmony with themselves, each other, and their environment. Another way of saying this more simply is that people are innately inclined to being healthy and happy. This potential is realized for each person according to the conditions that he is born into and finds during the rest of his life.

Conditions of oppression directly affect people's power. Since these conditions vary greatly for different people all over the world, it follows that the development of people's power will vary greatly as well. To the extent that a person's potential for a satisfying life is not realized, we call his state of being alienation, or powerlessness. Alcoholism is an extreme example of powerlessness and alienation in which a person cannot control harming his body with a dangerous substance.

Alienation

Alienation refers to a condition in which people are estranged from their powers. Alienation tends to affect certain specific sources of power: our hearts, our minds, our hands, and our bodies. It also affects people's socially based power; the power that comes from living, loving, and working together with others.

Lovelessness, the alienation from our heart, or love: We become alienated from our hearts, or our capacity to love each other and to relate to each other in a satisfying way. Our natural tendencies to love, to appreciate, to cooperate with, and to help each other are thwarted from early on.

We are taught the rules of the Stroke Economy which effectively reduces the amount of strokes or positive interaction between people. The Stroke Economy is a set of rules, supported by strong social sanctions which are taught to people from early in life. These rules seek to reduce the exchange of strokes between young and old, married and unmarried, men and men, women and women, and so on. In addition, they enjoin people not to give strokes that they might want to give, not to ask for or accept strokes they would like to get, not to reject unwanted strokes and not to give themselves strokes. The rules are taught and enforced primarily to "protect" the society from sexual excesses, even though strokes are not necessarily sexual. The combined effect of the Stroke Economy's rules is that strokes become artificially scarce and costly commodities instead of being freely available.

As a consequence of the Stroke Economy, we feel unloved and unlovable. We feel incapable of loving. We become sad, isolated, and depressed. We don't love humankind and fail to act in each other's behalf. We learn that we cannot allow someone else to become close or trust others with our hearts, and we fail to learn how to deal with the normal ups and downs of our relationships.

For a more thorough discussion of the Stroke Economy, see

Readings in Radical Psychiatry [3] and "Trashing the Stroke Economy" by Bob Schwebel.[4]

Mindlessness; the alienation from our minds, or capacity to think: We all have the capacity to develop our minds to understand the workings and facts of our world, to predict the outcome of events, and to solve problems. This capacity has been developed to a large degree by some poeple and becomes unavailable to others who, in their alienation from their minds, are incapable of thinking in an orderly way. Some people cannot keep thoughts fixed in their consciousness long enough to combine them with other thoughts to derive logical conclusions. Some people's consciousnesses become invaded with chaotic ideas which cannot be controlled. Complete confusion and the utter terror of mental breakdown are the extreme form of this kind of alienation, which tends to be diagnosed by the psychiatric establishment as "schizophrenia." Those who suffer from mind alienation are dealt with in the harshest and most unjust manner. Tranquilizing medication, shock therapy, imprisonment, and other cruel and punitive methods have been used over the years since psychiatry, the art of soul-healing, was usurped from all the legitimate practitioners of the art by the medical establishment. Padded cells, straitjackets, hot- and cold-water treatments, forced feeding, experimentation with dangerous drugs, and brain surgery have all been applied to people who have shown extreme forms of alienation from their minds. These methods, whose principal effect is to terrorize people into submission so that they will temporarily conform to the expectations of their helpers, have proven, one by one, to be totally ineffectual in anything but sweeping the problem under the rug.

Alienation from our minds is a result of systematic lies and discounts. A discount occurs when someone denies the content of our experiences. If, in addition to being told that our experiences aren't valid, we are also fed false information in the form of lies, the systematic discounts and lies combine to make us experience an interference with our thinking functions which eventually can lead to total mental breakdown.

One particularly well-known form of alienation is what is called by establishment psychiatrists "paranoid schizophrenia," in which the natural intuitive awareness of the facts of our persecution, which some become keenly aware of, are systematically discounted by others who also often lie to explain away their oppressive behavior. Some people's accurate perceptions of oppression, persecution, and abuse are most often effectively squelched and ignored. But other people's perceptions evolve into large-scale obsessions which develop into systems which, when elaborated, become fantastic and unreal; at this point they are called "paranoid delusions." The important fact, however, is that the "paranoid delusions," no matter how fantastic, are always based on a kernel of truth, and that is why we say in Radical Psychiatry that "paranoia is a state of heightened awareness." Consequently we encourage the expression of peple's paranoid fantasies and seek their validation by willingly searching for the grain of truth in them.

Joylessness; the alienation from our bodies, or feelings: Our intimate relationship with ourselves, that is, with all parts of our bodies, is interfered with by a number of alienating influences. We are told that our minds or spirit are separate from our body or flesh and that our body is, in some manner, the lesser of the two. We are told that those who use their minds are the ones who deserve power. We are encouraged to ignore our body's perceptions of disease (mind over matter) and to deal with them through powerful drugs which temporarily eradicate the symptoms of dysfunction. We are told that bodily pleasures are a dangerous evil. We learn to deny our bodily experiences, which include our emotions, whether they be positive or negative. We are given adulterated food without nutritional value and told to ignore its side effects. Eventually this systematic attack creates an alienation which puts our bodies' functions and their experiences beyond our conscious control. As a consequence, our bodies, which are the vessel, the matrix of our aliveness, become complete strangers to us and seem to turn on us through illness, addictions to harmful amounts and kinds of foods and drugs, and through unexplained and seemingly perverted needs which we have no control over. We feel that we are sick, powerless over our cravings. We give up hope and commit slow or sudden suicide. Alcoholism is a prime example of this kind of alienation.

Alienation from our hands, or work: People have a natural desire for and capacity to enjoy productive labor. The pleasures of productive activity are taken from us in two major ways. We are separated from the products of our labor when we are forced to work at a small, seemingly meaningless portion of the product that we are creating. In addition, we are separated from the value of the product that we are helping to create by those who employ us and who eventually profit disporportionately from their own participation in the product's creation. Being separated from our products and from their value causes us to hate our work and to despise what we have produced. Our labor—the creative and productive capacity of our hands—is lost to us, and we come to feel unproductive, bored, aimless, lazy, and worthless failures.

The major source of labor alienation in the world is corporate monopoly capitalism which treats workers as replaceable cogs in a profit-making machine. Within this system, labor is divided to the point that the worker doesn't have any involvement in the final product and may not even know what it looks like. Furthermore, the value of what he produces is taken largely by the employer. And, to add insult to injury, some of those profits are used to further separate the worker from his products and the means to produce them. This is done through strikebreaking, automation, and the creation of multinational corporations which import and exploit Third World labor and set worker against worker.

The result is a pervasive hatred of work, lack of productivity, job-related illness and accidents, and a loss of awareness of the joys of work. People resign themselves to being unhappy at work and seek pleasure through recreation, which has in itself been taken over by an exploitative industry, bent on further separating the worker from his money.

As shown in these examples, alienation is always the result of some form of oppression, combined with a set of lies and mystifications which supposedly legitimize that abuse. Oppression and mystification combine with physical and personal isolation of people from each other to create alienation. Because of this, we say that alienation equals oppression plus mystification plus isolation:

ALIENATION = OPPRESSION + MYSTIFICATION + ISOLATION

Oppression: The oppression which causes alienation comes in the form of various systems which attack specific subgroups of people: the poor, workers, people of color, women, old people, children, gay people, fat people, short people, and so on. As a rule, oppression—and therefore alienation—is greatest for people who are most dispossessed.

Workers are oppressed by their employers. People of color are oppressed by white people. Women are taken advantage of by men. The rights of young and older people are usurped by and taken away by the middle-aged. We live in a society in which competition and the use of power are taught and valued as ideals. Consequently, most people automatically take advantage of their positions of power, whether they are based on wealth, ownership of land or a business, race, gender, or age. People often unwittingly infringe on the rights of those who are less powerful than they are, without a second thought and with full sanction of those around them.

Oppression is accomplished through manipulative power plays which are taught to people in a wide variety ranging from the very crude and physical to the very subtle and psychological. Power plays are designed to make people do what they would not do of their free will. Power plays can be detected, analyzed, and classified. The study of power and power plays is an essential aspect of understanding oppression and alienation.

Mystification: The perpetration of abuse is usually accompanied by some kind of explanation which supposedly justifies it. Corporations explain their abuse of workers by pointing out that the corporation (or its owners) did, after all, invent the process or own the machinery or pay the overhead which is essential for the manufacture of their product. Rich people take advantage of poor people while asserting that everyone has equal opportunities in this land of plenty, so that those who don't succeed are directly responsible for their failures. Landowners mystify peasants by claiming divine or private property rights to the land. White people claim that people of color are less intelligent, less creative, less productive, less motivated, and thereby try to explain their own unequal access to privilege.

Men justify their privilege over women with sexist arguments. Children are told that they are not complete human beings, and that they must obey grownups who know best. Old people are mystified with notions of aging, loss of vitality and productivity.

Gay people are told they are depraved and sick. Single people are made to feel that their singlehood is neurotic. Each system of oppression has a set of mystifications which justify the power abuse perpetrated on its victims.

Eventually, people actually come to believe the lies that are used to justify the power abuse that they suffer. When people have incorporated in their own consciousness the arguments that explain and legitimize their oppression, then the mystification and alienation are complete. People will no longer rebel against oppression, but instead will blame themselves for it, accept it, and assume that they are the source and reasons for their own unhappiness. In addition, they will apply their internalized oppression to everyone around them and enforce others' oppression along with their own.

The portion of our mind which accepts the mystifications and internalizes oppression is called the "Enemy." The Enemy constantly stands guard over our mystification and feeds us messages to bolster and reinforce our alienation. The Enemy tells us that we are not O.K.; that we are bad, stupid, ugly, crazy, and sick, and that we deserve—and are the cause of—our own unhappiness. The Enemy is a major obstacle in the achievement of people's power and the recapturing of our capacities to work, love, think, and be in touch with our bodies.

Isolation: Being separated from and unable to communicate with each other is essential to alienation. By ourselves, without the aid of others who are in similar circumstances, we are completely powerless to think through our problems or do anything about them. It is part of the American Dream that people should achieve and do what they must do as individuals in isolation. Only those achievements which we can claim entirely for ourselves are thought of as being worthy. As a consequence, we erect competitive barriers between each other. When we are together we do not trust each other, we do not share with each other, and we go at the tasks of our lives as separate individuals, each one with our separate projects, living quarters, transportation, and nuclear families. The cult of individualism, which is the source of our isolation, is a very useful mystification for those who exploit us.

Power in the World

The opposite of alienation is power in the world. This power is achieved by fighting each element of alienation in turn. Because of this we say that Power in the World equals Contact to deal with Isolation, Awareness to deal with Mystification, and Action to deal with Oppression. (Thanks are due to Hogie Wyckoff for naming Power in the World as the antithesis to alienation.)

POWER = CONTACT + AWARENESS + ACTION

Contact: In order to combat isolation, it is necessary for people to join hands and gain the power of working together and supporting each other in their common goals through cooperation.

Cooperative relationships are based on the assumption that everyone has equal rights. They are best conducted in an atmosphere where power plays are not allowed, where people do not keep secrets from each other, and where people do not Rescue each other. (See Chapter 13.)

Only when we work cooperatively in an organized, coherent effort is it possible for us to make true progress in the fight against alienation. No one person can accomplish power in the world as long as she stands by herself, whether alone or in a crowd. That is why we focus so intensely on group process.

Awareness: The expansion of consciousness—especially our understanding of the manner in which oppressive influences operate to diminish our power—is the essence of Awareness. Consciousness-raising is the acculation of information about the world and how it functions, and is an important continuing task in expanding one's power in the world. Awareness of the function of different forms of oppression, like racism, sexism, ageism, and the exploitation of consumers of food and drugs is an essential aspect of consciousness-raising.

Constructive criticism is a vital consciousness-raising technique. In this process, people will offer information to those who want to hear it concerning their behavior and how it affects others. People may also suggest how another person's behavior may be changed and corrected for the benefit of all. Constructive criticism is greatly

aided by self-criticism and assumes willingness in all who participate to accept and learn from other people's critical analysis.

Action: Action is the process whereby our awareness of things
that need to be changed is put into effect. Contact alone, or
Contact and Awareness, can lead to strong, increased subjective
feelings of power. However, objective power in the world is different from subjective feelings of power and cannot result from
Awareness or Contact alone. Awareness and Contact must be translated into some form of Action which changes the actual conditions
in a person's life. Action implies risk, and when a person takes risks,
he may need protection from the fears and actual dangers that can
result from that action. Potent Protection in the form of actual
alliances for physical or moral support are needed in effective
Action and are an essential aspect of Contact. Action, Awareness,
and Contact are the essential elements that together make it possible for people to reclaim their power and liberate themselves from
their scripts.

11

Joylessness

Observing a wide-awake, healthy baby can give us an excellent picture of uninhibited aliveness. Let us look closer at this state of being alive as a contrast to joylessness, the state of alienation from one's body, which is the topic of this chapter.

Unless there is some startling distraction, the baby's experiences will fade into each other in a smooth sequence of clearly recognizable feelings. Contentment and smiles will yield to intense concentration, which will make way for discomfort, perhaps leading to a quiver of the chin which breaks out into crying, involving much physical motion which then subsides into peaceful suckling and so on. The expressive behavior of the young child goes on without any inhibitions or blocks; it flows like water between a creek's banks; rushing, bubbling, cascading smoothly as it goes along. If the baby is interested in something, it will stare at it intensely. If it feels uncomfortable, it will react with its whole body until the feeling fades away to allow the next sensation to dominate awareness. This behavior will go from joyful to unhappy, from pleasurable to uncomfortable, from intense to relaxed—but always obviously so, and never shaded by any hesitation or doubt. Furthermore, the feelings are expressed without attempting to hide or mask them.

This direct expression of feeling does not continue for long. In time, every show of emotion will be affected. Intense curiosity will be disapproved of and interfered with, shows of unhappiness will be curbed, extreme joy will be disallowed, and, one after another, the totally open expression of emotions will be moderated and channeled. The baby loves mother's breasts and is allowed to suck on them and to play with them but, little by little, there will come the time when she will not be allowed to touch—let alone, taste—them. Eventually such pleasures will be banished from the child's mind.

Early in life, little boys and girls will be prevented from freely touching their own bodies, especially the genitals. Crying may be allowed for some time, but it will surely have to stop—especially if the child is a boy. Loud, uproarious, abandoned laughter may have to go as well. If the child feels pain, parents will quickly reach for the aspirin. Upset stomachs, headaches, colds, bruises—all will be medicated out of existence.

The squelching of bodily experience affects both pleasure and pain. Pleasurable experiences such as touching oneself, touching each others' soft parts, kissing, licking, sucking, smelling will be banned right along with the discomforts whenever possible. Eventually even the *thoughts* of such experiences will disappear.

To the extent that a person is alienated from his bodily experiences, I call his condition joylessness. Joylessness is the opposite of aliveness. It is the anticipation of death while living. The symptom of joylessness is lack of feelings (except as they break through their emotional blocks). A person with a joyless script seldom feels love in his heart. Experiences of anger are sudden and explosive because anger is denied until it brims over. He knows no subtle feelings of tenderness or melancholy, is not aware of subtle bodily sensations. These go on below the level of his awareness, and he is cut off from them.

Yet this person—most often a man—may think of himself as healthy and alive for years until the physical damage that his script has created becomes manifest in chronic illness, addiction, or utter loneliness.

Because of the culture's encouragement of the passionless, logical mental "masculine" mode of experience, men spend their middle years being encouraged in their joyless lives; and it isn't usually until they enter their forties that they begin to recognize—faintly—that something is askew. Why does alcoholism affect men over women four to one? The answer, in my mind, is that joylessness, one of the sources of alcoholism, is primarily a masculine script. The squelching of feeling which men are expected to exercise is far more extensive than what is expected of women, and that leads to the greater likelihood of drug abuse.

The squelching of feeling operates very much like the squelch control in Citizens Band radios, which can be set to cut out all incoming signals until they reach a certain intensity.

Figure 7A shows a normal sequence of feelings and their intensity. Figure 7B show what happens when the feelings are squelched. Everything below the squelch line is blotted out from consciousness. Figure 7A shows that in a day's time the person goes through a complex sequence of feelings. Yet when these are squelched to a certain level (Figure 7B) all that the person is aware of is a feeling of love in the morning, a burst of anger accompanied by physical discomfort in the evening. All other feelings are buried, as are their causes. Their consequences, however, remain. The cause of the physical discomfort continues to do whatever damage it does, the reasons for anger go unaffected, the person will be seen to be heartless, and his heart will go without love.

The Corruption of Food

None of the possible physical pleasures that are available to people from early life are left untouched. Even the food that children are fed will be significantly adulterated. It will be intensely sugared and salted, shot through with artificial flavoring, preservatives, and coloring, and tainted with herbicides and pesticides (which are applied to all "normally grown" food) and contaminated with growth hormones and other chemicals (injected and fed into the animals that provide us with their meat). On one hand, therefore, all pleasures, feelings, and emotions are dampened and removed from our consciousness. On the other hand, the void that is left is filled by the tastes and the aftereffects of food and drink which are entirely contaminated with strong substances which are foreign to our bodies and many of which have already been proven to be addictive and harmful—if not deadly.

Many children grow into adults who are addicted to alcohol, cigarettes, and coffee; but even before that happens, children are hooked on sugar, artificial flavors, white flour, salt, and caffeine. Because they are universally accepted and promoted, these addictions are not even noticed. Similarly, many adults are dependent on strong chemicals to produce and maintain their well-being.

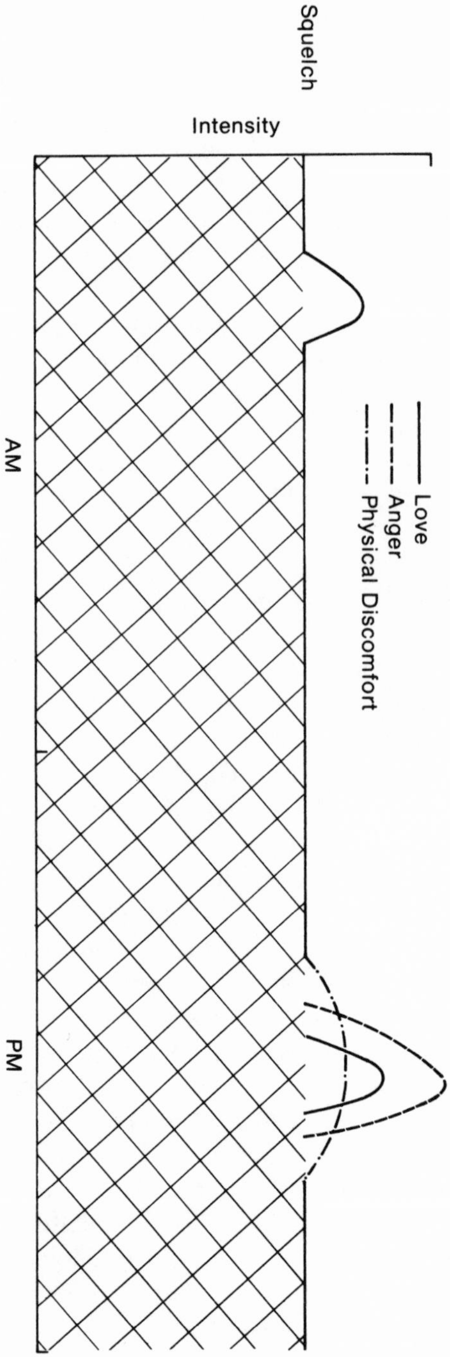

Figure 7B

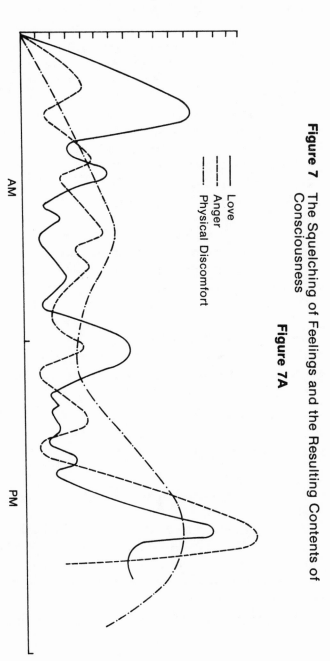

Figure 7 The Squelching of Feelings and the Resulting Contents of Consciousness

Figure 7A

Tranquilizers, sleeping pills, muscle relaxants, painkillers. From childhood these adults were encouraged to use aspirin, No-Doz, Sleep-Eze, Alka-Seltzer, Ex-Lax, cough syrup, nasal sprays and eye drops, to remedy their minor discomforts. The lesson we are taught is clear: "Don't feel (joy, anger, hurt, fear). Don't be excessively aware of pleasure or pain, and when you are in need of comfort, put something in your mouth which tastes good or will make you feel better."

When the discomfort is intense, alcohol will wipe it out effectively. Alcohol has brought joy into people's lives since time immemorial. It does so by chemically bringing down the squelch barrier that blocks feelings. Of course, alcohol alone is nòt the culprit. We know that in small quantities, taken at appropriate occasions, alcohol can add to the joys and health of an already joyful and healthy life. But when it is taken to make joylessness tolerable, alcohol becomes dangerous, because it will then be taken often and in large quantities. This kind of use will eventually lead to addiction.

As explained in previous chapters, the Enemy in the grown-ups that surround the child and eventually the Enemy in the child itself attacks spontaneous expression of feelings of pleasure and pain. By reducing spontaneity, it interferes with people's awareness of what goes on within their bodies; after years of expressionless living, people lose consciousness of their feelings. The Joylessness scripting keeps people emotionally illiterate, unable to know how and what they feel and therefore unable to express it.

Emotional Illiteracy

I have often compared my own "emotional illiteracy" to the difficulties I have when reading a Shakespeare play. I imagine that most people who read Shakespeare get general ideas of what is going on, but many of us miss the complexities, the nuances, the humor and the sense of tragedy. Some people who have trouble relating to literature as complex as Shakespeare's plays will decide that there is nothing to them, that they are just stupid and overblown. Others, including myself, realize that there is something missing in their understanding and will haltingly and painfully try to follow what is going on. And there are some people who are literate enough to be able to perceive what Shakespeare is conveying just by reading him.

Similarly, some people are emotionally literate and can "read" and understand the subtle language of the body, in themselves and others. Other people cannot; their own feelings often go unperceived and when they are noticed, are unclear and muddled. Only one's most blatant feelings are understood, and the feelings of others are similarly unclear and forgotten. Some others simply feel that emotions are unnecessary, self-indulgent and even stupid.

If we should suddenly become tuned into the events within our skins, we would become aware of a large number of happenings many of which we would find frightening, unacceptable, bizarre, and often amazing. People who are (for better or for worse) tuned in to the subtleties of their bodily experience and who, uncautiously, speak of them or act in their behalf at the wrong time, in the wrong place are in grave danger of being considered insane. We are wise not to speak too freely of the energies that travel through our bodies, of the fantasies that go on in our day- or sleeping dreams, of the sensations we feel in our hands and limbs, heads, hearts, and bellies, and of the kinds of things that really give us pleasure or pain.

I will speak later of body work and how, in the safe context of a body-work session, people who are encouraged to become aware of their bodily experiences will feel themselves expand or contract, flow into the air, sink into the ground. People will feel that they are bound by steel bands around their heads and chest, that their limbs are frozen, that their genitals are swollen or shriveled up, that they are soaring in space, or that they are dead inside.

In body work, people learn that these are their everyday experiences becoming conscious, that they are simply denied consciousness most of the time. Such experiences are often denied because they are considered abnormal. They must be kept to oneself lest one be taken off to the "nuthouse." And that fear is very real. Every one of the experiences that I describe above will be eyed with suspicion by the average psychiatrist; some of them are considered symptoms of mental illness.

I have already explained how avoiding bodily experiences makes us unaware of their existence. Because we are unaware of our own bodily feelings we also eventually become unaware of them in others. I have also mentioned that people who become anesthetized to their own internal experience will feel O.K. until some particular experience breaks through the squelching mechanism in the form of extreme feelings of anger, shame, fear, love, or joy, only to be quickly repressed and brought back to "normal."

The "normal" unfeeling experience is one of emptiness, vacuum, joylessness; it leaves us unexplainably and deeply dissatisfied. To fill the void, we seek stimulation which is strong and capable of breaking through the barrier. We find strong stimulation in fast-paced, loud music, violence, speeding, pornography, overeating, spending money; and, above all, we find it in drugs. Drugs punch through the body barrier and temporarily reestablish contact with the bodily experience. Unfortunately, the contact is brief, followed by the harmful and painful aftereffects of the drug. Then the barrier goes up again, only to be brought down again by larger doses of the drug.

Drug abuse keeps us emotionally illiterate. We never have to deal with the barriers that estrange us from our own personal experiences. We wind up having to pay the drug dealer, the bartender, the liquor-store owner, or the physician to get back snatches of our own experience, which has been alienated from us and which is kept alienated from us in the process.

Emotional illiteracy is the consequence of Critical Parent injunctions (Don't cry, Don't laugh, Don't be angry, Don't touch, etc.) and attributions (Be perfect, Be strong, Be happy, etc.). Fortunately, emotional literacy can be learned just like reading, writing, and arithmetic. Just as in the case of the 3 R's, it is easier to teach the young child than the grown-up who has developed many compensatory bad habits.

Teaching emotional literacy to an alcoholic typically involves giving permission to go against injunctions and attributions which are found in all people, but which seem to be strongest in people who abuse drugs. Group therapy and body work are ideal settings for people to learn how to feel and show anger, shame, love, affection and other emotions. Because of the agreement between group members to be supportive allies, a feeling of safety and trust develops which makes it easier to relax, open up, and show one's true self.

The next section of this book will be devoted to what can be done to heal alcoholism.

PART TWO

Healing Alcoholism

12

Myths of Alcoholism

There are many theories about what causes alcoholism, but precious few specific approaches to the problem. Alcoholics Anonymous remains the only choice for people who find themselves in difficulties with alcohol; and except for some of the specific recommendations made in my book, *Games Alcoholics Play*, I see very little that has been added that provides a practical approach to this bedeviling affliction. Most of the literature is filled with theoretical statements, shot through with ten-dollar words like "compulsion," "regression," "passivity," "latent homosexuality," "dependency," "psychosis," and so on. All these terms serve only to insult alcoholics and do not seem to answer the main question: "What do we do to help the alcoholic?"

As a result of this poverty of approaches, it is very difficult for an alcoholic to obtain reasonably competent treatment. Many therapists feel afraid and uncomfortable with alcoholics and are therefore reluctant to get into therapy with them. The more experienced therapists will happily refer alcoholics to other therapists while they keep the more pleasant clients for their own comfortable practices.

In this section I aim to provide psychotherapists with a set of guidelines for the therapy of alcoholism. These guidelines will also be of interest to the spouses, relatives, and friends of alcoholics, since they can be used, with a few modifications, by anyone who wants to relate to an alcoholic in a helpful way. But first, let's briefly explore certain myths about alcohol and alcoholism. These myths have served to obscure the obvious in a field which has been

riddled with contradictory opinions and points of view. Disposing
of them can clear the way for a sensible and effective approach.

"Alcoholism Is Just an Illness"

As we have seen, the notion of alcoholism as an illness (in the
sense that the medical profession defines illness) is an obstacle to its
proper treatment. It is important not to confuse illness which is a
consequence of excessive drinking with excessive drinking itself,
which is not an illness at all. Saying that alcoholism is an illness
(because of the different illnesses that are associated with it, like
delirium tremens, heart disease, or liver or brain disease) is like
saying that driving recklessly is an illness because it often leads to
broken bones and concussions which are treatable only by physicians.

On the other hand, alcoholism is a disease in a more general
sense. From the point of view of modern holistic medicine, which
regards disease in a completely different light than Western al-
lopathic (drug- and surgery-centered) medicine, any disturbance of
bodily functioning—and thus alcoholism—is a health disturbance.
Holistic medicine's specific treatment of alcoholism bears no re-
semblance to what has been the traditional medical approach.
Above all, sedatives and tranquilizers are not used. Instead, diet
and life-style changes are recommended, together with an expectation of the alcoholic's participation in the healing process. The
approach outlined in this book, and even its title, are strongly
influenced by holistic health ideas.

Attempts to treat alcoholism with drugs have failed, even
though at certain points of a drinking episode it might appear that
certain drugs can help. However, at this moment, there are no
drugs that specifically affect alcoholism, nor are there any drugs
that show any promise. In fact, it is my opinion that drugs for
alcoholics should be avoided altogether—except for medical emer-
gencies. It is important that alcoholics and their therapists abandon
the notion that alcoholism and medicine are necessarily related in
any way except in the very terminal stages of alcoholism when it
has become intimately associated with bodily tissue damage.

The sense that the alcoholic is progressively incurably ill and that therefore nothing can be done about the illness, except to keep the bottle corked, is as much a myth as the other extreme of thinking, which states that alcoholism is strictly a matter of choice.

"Alcoholism Is Just a Choice"

This myth lies beneath the notion that the alcoholic *chooses* to be an alcoholic and that the remedy is simply a matter of choosing otherwise. According to this view, the alcoholic doesn't need therapy, A.A., or any help at all. All she needs to do is make her mind up not to drink. This approach overlooks the many pressures under which the alcoholic finds herself and how those pressures are, at times, irresistible. It is an approach that leads to callousness on the part of the helper; nothing but the alcoholic's will to drink or not to drink is considered of any importance.

Only someone who has never been under the compulsion of drug or other substance abuse can understand how humiliating and persecutory such a point of view can be. Some alcoholics are so browbeaten by this view that they will accept and promulgate it themselves: "I am just a weak-willed person. All I have to do is stop drinking—then I'll stop being an alcoholic." Or "I have to do it myself—that's all there is to it" are the kinds of things alcoholics who have been thus indoctrinated will say about themselves. These views are not very useful; they sound brave and responsible, but they don't help because they are unrealistically simple. They result in nothing more than guilt and further feelings of powerlessness because they ignore the powerful factors other than choice that are the causes of alcoholism (addiction, habit, social pressures, the Enemy, etc.).

"Alcoholism Is Just a Symptom"

This point of view, which is shared by many therapists, is that drinking is merely a symptom of a psychological problem. As a consequence, these therapists will choose not to discuss the drinking (because it is merely a symptom) but will attempt to investigate its origins (childhood traumas, script injunctions and attributions, early family constellations, emotional conflicts, or repressed primal screams) through a variety of techniques such as psychoanalysis, gestalt therapy, or psychodrama—all of which ignore the everyday realities of the alcoholic's drug use. These therapists will have to deal with clients who are almost always under the influence of alcohol, or between binges, and cannot realistically exercise enough common sense and Adult control to deal with whatever they must do from day to day to make their lives work.

Transactionally speaking, the therapist who chooses to ignore the client's drinking in favor of dealing with his basic conflicts is playing the role of Rescuer (Patsy variety) in the game of Alcoholic and thus is contributing to the continuation of the problem. Regardless of whether drinking is a symptom or not, it is necessary and desirable that the alcoholic stop drinking as the very first step in therapy. Stopping the drinking may not be a cure, but it does stop the progression of the script and is thus an indispensable move. Only a reliably sober person can find the energy and clarity of mind necessary to deal with the underlying causes of alcoholism. Regarding alcoholism as only a symptom can be a major mistake comparable to forgetting to bail out a sinking boat while looking for the leaks.

Allied with the misconception that alcoholism is just a symptom of deep underlying emotional conflicts is the assumption that only "deep" one-to-one individual psychotherapy can be effective in dealing with it. The idea that effective psychotherapy of alcoholism can only be done by bearded gentlemen in dollar-a-minute, daily or biweekly fifty-minute sessions is a logical consequence of such a belief. Actually, alcoholism is not as deep as all that; neither in fact, is any other psychological major or minor disturbance. How deep and ominous any one emotional affliction is thought to be seems to be directly related to the practitioner's ignorance about it. Schizophrenia, manic-depressive psychosis, drug dependency are deep, frightening, ominous-sounding names given to serious human problems by professionals who don't know what to do about them.

In my experience, none of these "deep" "mental illnesses" requires heroic methods of therapy. They require only a relaxed, nurturing, well-informed, experienced, and optimistic approach. Accordingly, group psychotherapy has proved to be every bit as effective as one-to-one therapy—especially in the treatment of alcoholics. In groups, alcoholics seem more capable of ridding themselves of the problem permanently than in "deep" one-to-one analysis.

In summary: alcoholism isn't one single problem. Instead, it is the result of a combination of physical, personal, and social factors which exist in different people at different times in their lives. When the "right" combination occurs—and it occurs in about twenty million people in this country at this time—alcoholism results. What can be done about it will be discussed in the rest of this book.

13

The First Step:
Getting the Contract

Most of us have a healthy desire to nurture and take care of people who need us. Many of us have also had the experience of starting out as helpers and rescuers—and winding up the victims of the very person we are trying to help. The classic example is the innocent bystander who is walking on the beach and sees someone drowning. He jumps in, swims up to the victim, and, in the process of rescuing him, drowns right along with him—though sometimes the victim, ironically, survives. Many of the techniques lifeguards learn are designed precisely to prevent their being drowned by a drowning swimmer. Similarly, a person who is interested in helping other needs to develop effective techniques for helping; techniques which need to include safeguards against being dragged down and destroyed by the very ones she aims to help.

Alcoholics, especially, seem to have the knack of attracting the good graces of people who start out feeling that they can help and wind up totally swamped. This situation is characterized in Transactional Analysis as a Rescue. Rescue, is one of the roles in the games of Alcoholic and must be avoided at all costs by anyone who intends to be helpful to the alcoholic. The reasons are many; not the least of them is that it certainly does not help to be drawn in and brought to the level of emotional disorganization that tends to be characteristic of the alcoholic's life.

In this connection, it is helpful to distinguish between a small "r" rescuer and a capital "R" Rescuer. The rescuer is someone who as part of his vocation or avocation helps people in distress. Among such are lifeguards, firefighters, police officers, physicians, nurses, social workers, and so on. It is quite possible to be effective as a rescuer and truly benefit other people in need. On the other hand, rescuers can also be Rescuers; people who get caught in the Rescue game with a Victim.

When a rescuer becomes a Rescuer, he steps into the merry-go-round of the Drama Triangle. He becomes an actor in a play and loses his potency as a healer. His behavior will cease to be therapeutic; his words will become lines read from a script which serve only to promote the alcoholic's tragedy through to the final curtain.

The basic difference between a rescuer and a Rescuer is relatively easy to detect. Anyone who wishes to avoid playing the game or Rescue need only to make sure of the following:

Don't do more than 50 percent of the work or invest more than half the effort in any situation in which you are helping someone; even God in His infinite mercy won't—or so the saying goes. It doesn't make any sense to try to help those who won't help themselves. It is important to only go halfway in any situation in which we are trying to be helpful.

That means, first and foremost, that we do not help someone who is not asking for help. Diving headfirst into situations where the victim hasn't even asked to be saved is the most blatant example of a Rescue. Alcoholics are expert at presenting us with a situation which is in need of repair. They may not want to commit themselves to working on it, but they're quite willing to let us try if we want to. Characteristically, the alcoholic's helper does most of the talking, cooking, traveling, staying awake, planning, or thinking while the alcoholic simply does most of the drinking. To avoid this aspect of the Rescue, it is essential that anyone who intends to truly help an alcoholic arrive at a contract (discussed later in this chapter) and stick to it faithfully.

Very often we begin a helping relationship with love in our hearts and a true desire to help. In certain situations, this desire remains part of our motivation and we continue to want to help. Very often, however, our desire to help diminishes and eventually disappears while it suddenly appears that we are now compelled to go on helping whether we like it or not.

In a reasonable helping situation, we are able to make as much of a contribution as we want to make for as long as we want to. We remain free to withdraw and let the person help himself or find others to help him.

Not so in a Rescue. A Rescue is like a fishhook; once we take the bait, it is very hard to let go. We cannot stop the Rescue because we develop the impression that our Victim will drown, fall apart, die, or kill himself if we do. We are stuck because we do not want to be responsible for the tragic end of another person. Somehow, in the process, our Victim has shifted the responsibility for his condition entirely onto our shoulders. Because we are reasonable, humane human beings, we cannot simply dump him—so we unwilling carry the load sometimes through extraordinarily long and arduous periods of time.

This may come as a shock to you, but if you helping an alcoholic and find yourself really not wanting to do it anymore and don't stop soon, you will be Rescuing. If you *are* Rescuing, you are not only *not* helping the alcoholic, you are actually harming her. This is true for anyone—whether she works in an agency dealing with alcoholics or is in a relationship with an alcoholic—as a child, spouse, or parent. If you are helping without the desire to help, or if you are doing more than your share of the work, you are not only not being helpful, you are making the problem worse.

This is difficult for people who may be totally immersed in Rescuing an alcoholic to believe. But it is true. I have witnessed scores of situations in which, after forcefully pointing this out to a Rescuer and insisting that he stop the Rescue, the alcoholic did not go under, die, or commit suicide, but in fact pulled himself together and made some improvement in his life. How people can extricate themselves from a Rescue will be covered in Chapter 16. In the following pages, I want to show how a good contract prevents Rescues.

Drawing up a contract is the indispensable first step in effective alcoholism therapy. Transactional Analysis is a contractual form of group treatment which must be distinguished from other activities that may be of therapeutic value. A person may do all sorts of things alone or in groups which could presumably be helpful. Going to a football game or a dance, joining an encounter group, spending a weekend in the woods meditating or beginning psychoanalysis are all activities that might be helpful. The basic difference between these activities and a Transactional Analysis group is the contract.

Therapeutic contracts—contracts between a person who holds herself out to be a competent therapist and a client—should be regarded with as much respect as legal contracts in a court of law. Two aspects of legal contracts are fully applicable to therapeutic contracts: (1) informed mutual consent; (2) consideration. These requirements were developed over hundreds of years, so it is reasonable to accept them as pragmatically effective as well as socially desirable in the establishment of a therapeutic contract.

Informed Mutual Consent

Mutual consent implies that both of the parties in a contract are consciously and sincerely agreeing to the terms of the contract. Therapeutic consent implies the request, offer, and acceptance of therapy. Presumably, the client has come to the therapist to get help for her condition. Presumably also, the therapist understands the situation and is willing to make a contribution to the improvement of that condition.

In order to make an informed, intelligent offer, the therapist should clearly understand the client's specific situation and what the client wants to change. In order for the acceptance to be informed, the client needs to understand what the therapist requires as conditions for the therapy; consequently, the therapeutic offer should contain a clear description of the conditions which the therapist considers essential for the process to be successful and how success will be defined.

Establishing mutual consent as part of the contract is particularly relevant to the therapy of alcoholics, since it is not unusual for an alcoholic to be accustomed to and willing to enter into a therapeutic relationship without any contract at all. For example, it is common for alcoholics to get into therapy as a result of pressures applied by family or by the courts. A therapist may mistakenly assume that there is mutual consent in the ensuing relationship when, in fact, the client is not willingly involved but instead feels coerced and victimized in the situation. On the other hand, it is also typical in the therapy of alcoholics that a willing

client blindly agrees to entering the situation without any understanding of what its requirements are—only to find out later that
the requirements are far different than expected.

My experience is that the minimum requirements for successful
therapy with alcoholics are as follows:

1. Complete sobriety for a minimum of a year during which

2. The client attends group therapy regularly every week for
two hours and

3. Involves himself in specific homework including diet and
other life-style changes addressed to his specific problems and

4. Attends my monthly body-work sessions

The establishment of a mutual informed-consent relationship
involves three transactions:

1. The request for treatment from the client,

2. An offer of treatment by the therapist and

3. An acceptance of treatment by the client.

It is not unusual in the relationships between therapist and
client for them to enter into therapy without these three elements
having been fulfilled. Look at the following conversation between
Jack, an alcoholic, and Jill, a therapist:

Jill: what can I do for you, Jack?

Jack: I'm here to get therapy.

Jill: Fine. I have an opening available for you on Tuesday at six
o'clock. Can you make it?

Jack: Yes, I can. I guess I'll see you on Tuesday.

This conversation may seem to achieve mutual informed consent. If examined closely, however, it may turn out that the client's
request was really only as follows:

Jill: What can I do for you, Jack?

Jack: (My wife is leaving me and I was arrested for drunk
driving and my mother, the judge, and my wife say that I need to
get into therapy, so) I am here to get therapy.

This is not really a request for therapy, and it is definitely the
beginning move in a Rescue game. It would be a great mistake for a

therapist to agree to work with a person under the above circumstances. Let's try again.

Jill: What can I do for you, Jack?

Jack: I'm here to get therapy.

Jill: Why do you want therapy?

Jack: Well, I guess I need it.

Jill: Maybe you don't need it. What makes you think you do?

Jack: Well, I'm drinking too much, and I'm getting sick. My wife is going to leave me, and I may have to go to jail for drunk driving. I want to stop drinking because it is ruining my life. Do you think you can help me?

Jill: Yes, I think I can. I have an opening available for on Tuesday at six o'clock. Can you make it?

Jack, Yes, I can. I guess I'll see you on Tuesday.

This example involves a request for therapy, but it doesn't involve a proper offer because the therapist has not stated what she intends to do or what she hopes to accomplish. She hasn't really got the information to understand whether she can actually help, and she has not stated her conditions for helping. Thus they are both still considerably in the dark with respect to informed mutual consent.

The therapeutic offer by the therapist implies that she understands the problem, that she is willing to deal with it, and that she has reasonable expectations to be successful in the process,

In order for informed mutual consent to occur, the therapist needs to have certain information. In my experience, the following facts must be investigated before a therapist can enter into a therapeutic contract with a client.

Does the person recognize himself to be an alcoholic? As I explained in Chapter 1, this question means: Does the person feel that his drinking is out of control and/or that it is harming him? Jack has indicated that he recognizes both: he feels that his drinking is out of control and that it is harming him.

If a person with a "drinking problem" asks for therapy but does not see his drinking as being out of control or harmful, it is important to examine the extent of the drinking. The following questions are useful:

What kind of alcohol and in what quantities does the person drink? This question needs to be answered in detail. No vagueness should be allowed. If the amount the person drinks varies, an average for a typical week should be obtained. A person who drinks more than two ounces a day regularly or who drinks more than five ounces within a period of two hours more than once every three months can be considered a problem drinker.

When does the drinking occur? Anyone who drinks before lunch and everyone who drinks regularly in the evening can be considered a problem drinker. On the other hand, a person may drink what seems imprudent amounts at usual times and not really have an alcoholic problem though he may be in danger of developing one.

For instance, a person may regularly drink before going to sleep. She may be using alcohol as a sleeping medication; it is a reasonable substitute for some other form of drug. While this is definitely a problem, it isn't necessarily a problem of alcoholism, but it may be as a problem of insomnia. When a drug is taken just for its purely physical biochemical effects, it lacks the social and psychological aspects of alcoholism. It will be easier to deal with and will require a different approach than the usual alcoholic problem.

If the therapist has adequate information about the client's drinking, she can now involve herself in mutual, informed consent. If the client shows signs of alcoholism and sees himself as having an alcoholic problem, she is now in a position to make an offer. Consider the following:

Jill: What can I do for you, Jack?

Jack: I am drinking too much and I am getting sick. My wife is going to leave me, and I may have to go to jail for drunk driving. I want to stop drinking because it is ruining my life. Do you think you can help me?"

Jill: Okay, Jack, I think I can help you. Let me tell you what is involved. If you get into therapy with me, I have certain expectations of you. In order for it to work, you need to come to group meetings every week for a two-hour session and to body-work meetings once a month. You need to attend regularly. This kind of therapy doesn't work while you are drinking, so it is necessary that you stop drinking altogether as soon as possible and that you don't drink at all for at least one year. During that year, in addition to attending group regularly, I expect you to be actively involved in working to solve your problem and that will include doing homework on diet and life-style changes between meetings. So if you come to group regularly, don't drink for a year and we work together on your problem, I expect that you will be cured of your alcoholism. If you are willing to agree to this, we can proceed.

I have an opening available for you on Tuesdays at six o'clock.

Jack: Okay, I understand, I will see you on Tuesday.

This highly condensed example contains three requirements for mutual informed consent: a request, an offer, and an acceptance. It is a model for a successful beginning contract which is likely to result in satisfactory work to both of the parties (client and therapist) as well as the other members of the group.

On occasion, an individual seeking therapy is clearly an alcoholic, but wants to work on some other difficulty. For example, Jack may want to work on his relationship with his wife but may wish to leave his drinking alone. Making an offer to treat a relatively minor disturbance such as marital disharmony, without dealing with the alcoholism, is a mistake that will surely lead to difficulties. It can be compared to being willing to perform plastic surgery on a terminal patient and should be declined on th ground that the alcoholism is so disruptive in itself that it will defeat any efforts to deal with some other minor disturbance. Unless the therapist wants to face unending frustration and difficulties, such a request should be politely denied with a frank explanation.

However, on occasion, a person may come to therapy with a drinking problem that is not severe enough to be called alcoholism. Under those circumstances, it is best to take a "wait-and-see" attitude. It is possible to make a temporary short-term contract to deal with some minor difficulty and pursue the alcohol situation to see whether the drinking is serious enough to require a primary contract dealing with alcoholism.

On occasion, drinking difficulties are really minor and fade away as other problems are dealt with. I am always willing to give clients the benefit of the doubt and take some time to see how severe their alcoholism really is.

The Consideration

A helper gives of himself. To avoid a Rescue, the person helped needs to give something in return. In legal terms, this is called the consideration.

Every contract must be based upon a valid consideration. Valid consideration refers to benefits that pass between the therapist and the client. These benefits may be bargained for and eventually agreed upon. The benefit conferred by the therapist should always be a competent attempt to remedy the disturbance. In exchange, the client will usually pay the therapist money. But money is not the only kind of benefit a client can confer upon the therapist. Let us look at the consideration in some detail.

As stated above, the benefit conferred by the therapist should be a remedy to the disturbance. That is why it is important that the client clearly states the way her life is unsatisfactory and what would be required for satisfaction. The client needs to state specifically what is making her unhappy. Is she drinking too much? Is she unable to sleep? Does she cry all the time? Does she fail to have good relationships? Is she hated by her friends? Is she unable to keep a job? and so on. She should also be able to state what would make her life satisfactory. Getting a job and keeping it, being in a reasonably happy love relationship, being able to sleep and wake up refreshed and happy, getting rid of headaches, or stopping drinking.

The therapist has delivered his consideration in the contract when the person, the therapist, and the majority of the members in the group agree that the problem described in the beginning of therapy is no longer present. That is why, at the beginning of therapy, problems need to be stated in clear, behavioral, simple, observable terms, understandable to an eight-year-old. Without this initial statement, it is impossible to determine whether the problem has been solved.

On the other hand, the consideration given by the client can vary. The most common consideration in the therapeutic contract is money, but it is also possible to barter for goods or services which would satisfy the therapist's needs. When entering into a barter agreement, it is very important for the therapist to feel that the value received is equivalent to what he ordinarily expects from a client. Consequently, bartering must be done very thoughtfully and should always be left open to revision or revocation, since it is not uncommon for barter arrangements to remain satisfactory as a consideration for the therapist.

People who wish to help an alcoholic as friends rather than as therapists need to be equally scrupulous about mutual consent and consideration involved in the relationship. In addition to making it clear that the alcoholic wants our help and is willing to work at least as hard as we are on his problem, it is also important that we get something in return (not necessarily of a material sort) for our effort. If you are my friend, and if I am willing to speak to you on the phone for an hour about your problem, then I expect you will be willing to listen to me for an hour at some future date should I need it. If I come to your house and help you clean up a mess you made, then I expect you to do a similar favor for me should the need arise. I will make an effort to ask you for your help so that we keep the balance of energy devoted to each other more or less even. If I lend you money, I expect you not only to return it but to lend me money or something that I need when I need it. If I give my help to you freely I expect you to give help equally elsewhere. The equation of energy-in/energy-out has to maintain some semblance of balance between us or we will slip into a Rescue game and I will inevitably become angry with you, cease to have an interest in helping you, and may eventually persecute you.

People who "selflessly" help others while expecting nothing in return are weakening the effectiveness of their help. At the very least, a helper can expect an energetic effort to change a willing- ness to work hard, and an eagerness to learn. To many helpers, this type of positive attitude is sufficient consideration for their work. If so, well and good—it is the very least that should be expected. To expect more is reasonable; in any case the consideration must be made fully clear and should be negotiated for maximum success.

The Alcoholic Treatment Contract

As I have mentioned earlier, every alcoholic's first task is to stop drinking. Therefore this is also the first contract. However, it does not need to be the only contract. As long as he is drinking it is foremost in importance; but obviously, when the drinking ceases, other matters have to be attended to: his personal life, his work, recreation, health habits, nutrition. Consequently, an alcoholic in therapy will have additional contracts, such as:

Finding a better job
Getting strokes
Stop eating sugar (or drinking coffee) (or smoking) (or all three)
Make friends
Improve sex life
Fight the Enemy
Stop Rescuing
Develop an Ally
Give more strokes
Be truthful
Show feelings
And so on.

For some people, completing a contract such as "Showing my feelings" can represent a couple of years' work which results in a change of life-style that includes giving up alcoholism. Other contracts, such as "Find a better job," can be one of a series of contracts which the client chooses during her therapy.

For effective therapy, a client needs to have a contract *throughout.* As each contract gets worked through, the question becomes: "Is therapy complete, or should we start on another contract?" The answer to this question is up to the client rather than the therapist. Any new contract should be made with the same scrupulous attention to mutual involvement as the last. Therapists need to look out for that common tendency in our profession which compels us to tell our clients what they should (or shouldn't) do. This is essential to ensure that any contracts arrived at are based on the needs and desires of the client rather than the therapists. This is not to say that the therapist should not freely express his opinions on this or any other matter—only that these opinions should take a back seat to the client's needs and opinions.

The Cooperative Contract

In addition to the specific personal contract that each client works on there is another contract in my groups which involves all the group members, including the therapist: the Cooperative Contract. This contract specifies that there shall be no Rescues, no lies, and no power plays among the participants.

Rescues have been amply covered so far; let me briefly explain what is meant by no lies or secrets and no power plays. A more complete description of these two concepts can be found in *Scripts People Live.*[1]

No lies or secrets: Everyone in the group agrees to complete truthfulness. This means no deliberate untruths or lies of commission are told, and that includes lies of omission as well. If a group member who has been drinking is asked about it and denies it, this is a lie of commission. But if she is not asked and fails to mention it, she is lying as well. According to this definition, a lie is the deliberate act of hiding what someone else wants to know. Clearly, in a group-therapy situation, everyone wants to know whether an alcoholic member is drinking.

This rule applies also to the hiding of feelings, desires, or opinions. If a person is angry or has loving feelings for someone else in the group, not expressing these feelings is keeping a secret. Similarly, not expressing desires or critical opinions is a form of lying as well. Truthfulness involves asking for 100 percent of what one wants 100 percent of the time.

No power plays: A power play is a transaction designed to manipulate another person into doing something she or he would not otherwise do. Accordingly, people cannot intimidate, bully, threaten, or yell at each other to get desired results. Nor can they try to get the same result by sulking, guilt-tripping, or withdrawing from the group. Especially important is the application of this rule to the therapist's behavior; many of the "motivating" tricks that therapists feel free to use are not allowed in a cooperative problem-solving group. For example, according to the cooperative contract, it is not permissible to pretend to be angry and to insult someone in order to help him get angry and express his feelings. That would be both a lie and a power play to boot.

This contract is especially useful to stimulate the full expression of feelings. It encourages the honest expression of opinions and feedback. It is an ideal testing ground for asking for what one wants and for not Rescuing. It provides the necessary trust and feelings of safety that are essential for the open and honest discussion of all the facets of one's life right down to the most embarrassing. The cooperative contract, together with each member's individual contracts, are a powerful social structure within which people can radically improve their lives.

14

Sobriety

After making a contract, a person who has decided to deal with her alcoholism must concentrate on stopping the use of alcohol altogether. Most people who are alcoholic realize that they have become powerless over alcohol and that the best approach to their problem is to stop drinking entirely. This realization is arrived at through an honest evaluation of the lack of success of previous attempts to deal with their drinking. Many people with drinking problems have also had contact with Alcoholics Anonymous and have come to see the one universally accepted truth in alcoholism work: You can't fight alcoholism while you are drinking.

People who have come to accept this commonsense fact are at a distinct advantage over those who still hope that they can deal with their alcoholism without giving up alcohol.

Nevertheless, there will be people who will want to cut down their drinking instead of stopping altogether. They usually have not seriously tried to stop drinking and imagine themselves still in control. When a person insists that he wants to try to deal with his alcoholism without abstaining entirely, it is very important for the therapist to respond effectively to this understandable desire. The most effective response is one which succeeds in communicating the very important facts of "cutting down" while drinking and at the same time avoid the parental, persecutory, uptight authoritarianism which alcohol workers usually use in that situation.

This is a good place to discuss the concept of loving confrontation: the ideal combination of therapeutic transactions which are

most effective in working with alcoholics and, indeed, in any inter-
personal working situation.

Loving Confrontation

A client who seeks therapeutic help chooses a certain therapist
presumably because he thinks that the therapist knows what she is
doing. Thus it makes sense that the client wants to be presented
with the facts as the therapist sees them. If the therapist thinks that
it is very difficult—if not impossible—to stop alcoholism by just
"cutting down," then presumably the client would like to hear
that, along with whatever other useful information the therapist
has.

However, alcoholic clients are often reluctant to accept the
therapist's conviction that they must stop drinking completely in
order to succeed. That reluctance may have more to do with the
way the information is transmitted than with the information itself.
Granted, alcoholics usually secretly hope to hear that it is possible
to have one's drink and beat alcoholism at the same time, but they
don't mind being confronted with the facts as long as the information is presented in an acceptable manner. Nobody likes to have
facts—no matter how correct—shoved down one's throat; unfortunately, therapists often give clients their opinions in a supercilious, parental, and generally obnoxious manner.

It is possible to present information from a strictly Adult, scientific perspective. In this case, the therapist might say:

"You know that 95.6 percent of the people who have attempted
to deal with their alcoholism without stopping entirely have failed.
It would seem that chances of 'cutting down' are practically nil."

This is a "Confrontation" statement coming from the Adult of
the therapist. It is certainly an improvement over this statement,
which comes from the Critical Parent:

"It is ridiculous for you to think that you can stop being alcoholic without stopping drinking entirely. I have never seen it done,
and I don't expect you to be the fit to do it. You'd better do it the
way everybody else does it. You can't afford to be special at this
point in your life."

This approach is liable to antagonize the client—and rightfully so, since it comes from the therapist's Enemy. Its wording and tone are going to stimulate the client's anger, guilt, shame, rebelliousness, or some other rational emotion, which can only lead to confusion and lack of success.

However, the proper mixture of factual confrontation with a nurturing emphasis and tone is the most effective in this situation:

"Look, I can understand that you would like to continue to drink on occasion while you are trying to overcome your problem. Unfortunately, I don't believe it can be done. (Nurturing) My experience shows that only a very small percentage has been able to do it (Confrontation) and while I am not necessarily sure that you can't, I just think it would be a lot easier if you stopped drinking altogether. (Nurturing) What do you think? Do you think you can cut down? I don't (Confrontation)."

Another approach might be: "Look, you may not realize this, but you are powerfully addicted to alcohol. (Factual Confrontation) You probably wish that this wasn't so, and that you could feel more powerful in the situation and just cut down. I can understand that very well, (Nuturing) but the fact is that it is virtually impossible to do that. (Confrontation) Why don't you make it easy on yourself and just stop altogether? I'd hate to see you spend the next three months in all that useless agony. (Nurturing)."

For anyone who is addicted, the notion of having to stop completely is usually quite frightening. After all, the drug offers some pleasure or relief, and life is hard enough without giving up what seems to be its major pleasures. More important, though, someone who is addicted fears that stopping completely and abruptly might be extremely difficult and could become a horrifying struggle, ending ultimately in failure. Nobody likes to appear incapable of controlling his own actions, and I believe that people who are addicted hate to accept the idea that they must stop completely in order to be successful, because it acknowledges their helplessness.

Fear of failure, the dread of being powerless and being shown up to other group members, family members and the therapist as lacking in will and self-control, are probably the main reasons that people won't struggle against their alcoholism. In addition, alcoholics don't often comprehend the magnitude of their addiction. Hence they blame themselves for their incapacity to stop, and they feel weak and gutless. Instead, they should realize that they are in

the jaws of a veritable steel trap. That is why a nurturing, understanding approach is essential. Therapists should not sit in judg-
ment. They need to be sympathetic to the plight of the addicted
person, and that sympathy is shown by avoiding a supercilious
parental attitude as well as a cold and unemotional Adult attitude
which simply serves up the facts without any feeling.

Information is important, but information alone does not con-
stitute the most effective form of therapy. On the other hand, love
is not enough either. Information and love are both powerful aspects of therapy, but they are most powerful when they are offered
to the person together in loving confrontation.

After mentioning the unlikelihood of success unless complete
sobriety is achieved for at least one year, it is important to negotiate the agreement between the therapist and the client. If the
client insists that she wants to "cut down," then I am usually
willing to give it a try with the understanding that her effort will be
evaluated after a few weeks. If it is not successful, I will insist that
she stop completely.

"Look, Mary, I have not seen this approach work with someone
as addicted as you, even though a lot of people want to try it to
begin with. But I'm not going to stand here and tell you that you
can't do it because you may be one of the few people who can.
Some people have stopped being alcoholics by just cutting back; I
have never experienced it. I'd rather you didn't, but, if you insist,
let's give it a try. Work at it for the next month. Let's say that you
will restrict yourself to a total of seven ounces of alcohol per week
for the next week. We will talk about how you are doing at the next
meeting, and I hope you succeed. Let's try it."

The client may want to drink a different quantity over a different period of time; that can be negotiated as long as the amount
that is consumed clearly qualifies as "social drinking." What is
important: an attempt is being made to cooperatively negotiate, on
the basis of the therapist's and the client's points of view. This
mutually respectful, cooperative approach may seem inefficient;
but, in the end, because it avoids power plays, it is the one that
builds the kind of trust and mutual respect that is essential for good
results.

Loving confrontation avoids Persecution on one hand and Rescues on the other. It is loving without being mindless, and it is

tough and confronting without being persecuting. It cultivates mutual love and respect. And it works.

Antabuse

Clients who recognize the importance of stopping drinking entirely and who expect difficulty can be helped with disulfiram (Antabuse). Many people accept this offer without hesitation. Antabuse is a drug which, in combination with even small quantities of alcohol, produces extremely uncomfortable symptoms. With a susceptible person, or if a lot of alcohol is taken, the alcohol-Antabuse combination can even lead to death.

Antabuse should be taken every day. Because it remains in the body for as long as seven days, it is an effective deterrent against the impulse to drink since drinkers have to plan days in advance if they wish to start drinking again.

Antabuse can be used in a number of ways, some of which are completely ineffective—if not harmful—in helping people overcome alcoholism. Most ineffective is forcing the alcoholic to take Antabuse either by putting it in his food or through a more subtle form of power play. This approach may work as long as the therapist or his agents are capable of forcing the drug into the client's body, but inevitably it will create antagonism and resentment. As soon as an opportunity presents itself, the client will be compelled, due to justifiable pride—if for no other reason—to go on a bender with all possible speed.

To illustrate the total ineffectiveness of this type of coercive approach to drug abuse, let's look at Jack, a borderline alcoholic who got into some alcohol-related trouble with the law. To his great shock, he landed in jail with a nine-month sentence. Jack is a reasonable man who understands that he has a drinking problem. He feels he needs to do something about it. During the nine months of incarceration, which was seen by the authorities as a period of "rehabilitation," he was forced to attend A.A. meetings and to take Antabuse. He was confined in a low-security institution where he might have had access to alcohol, and he took his Antabuse and attended A.A. meetings without protest.

Jack is a D&P player, and I expect him to eventually deal with the problem and stop drinking excessively. But throughout his incarceration, he said that the very first thing he would do once he got out of jail was stop taking Antabuse and get drunk. When I asked him why he would plan such a thing, since alcohol was a problem for him and that this might be a very bad way of using his freedom, he pointed out to me that it was a matter of simple pride and red-blooded American rebelliousness. He would deal with his alcoholism later—but the first thing he would do when he got out of jail was to get drunk, and there was no two ways about it. Jack spent the nine months that were supposed to serve as rehabilitation designed to launch him on a drug-free way of life, planning day by day and hour by hour how drunk he would get, what he would drink, and whom he would drink it with.

Forcing Antabuse (or any therapy) on people does not help, but Antabuse can be extremely helpful to a habitual drinker who wants to be rid of the constant, nagging temptation to drink which is so characteristic of the beginning stages of sobriety. Antabuse has no direct effect on the desire to drink; but because the possibility of drinking is completely excluded, it basically frees the alcoholic's consciousness from the ongoing struggle between his desire to drink, and his decision to stop. For some people, the elimination of this internal struggle can be a blessing; their minds can now be occupied with other matters, and drinking becomes a much less dominant thought, which has to be dealt with only on occasion and which gradually recedes in its power to flood consciousness without warning or control.

If over the first few months of sobriety, whenever the alcoholic thinks, "I want to have a drink," there is another, automatic thought that says, "Forget it—you'll get sick," the frequency and intensity of the desire to drink will be dramatically reduced. That does not mean that there will not be periods of time in which the alcoholic will have intense conflicts dealing with drinking and at which time he may consider not taking Antabuse so he can have a drink a few days later. But it can be clearly seen how this is a large improvement over the situation in which relief is only a swallow away.

This is how Antabuse is administered at the Center for Special Problems, a public health clinic in San Francisco. With very few exceptions, any person who wants Antabuse is prescribed the drug.

People who are refused usually have a recent history of its misuse or have a medical condition that makes an Antabuse reaction threatening—more threatening than alcoholism itself. After appropriate warnings, the drug is dispensed. No attempt is made to produce the Antabuse reaction in the clinic. The initial dosage is 500 mg. (1 tablet) per day for seven days, which is then cut down to 250 mg. per day. With this approach there have been no known deaths due to Antabuse, or severe reactions. A few patients will experiment by drinking a small quantity of alcohol. Most of them are quickly convinced of the drug's effectiveness and stop experimenting. On occasion, a patient reports such a small effect that he was able to continue drinking on top of Antabuse. In such cases, Antabuse therapy is discontinued.

Antabuse has a few unpleasant side effects, such as a strong garlicky breath, and this is another reason why people resist its use. These side effects can usually be eliminated by taking the daily dose just before going to sleep at night, and by reducing the dosage to 125 mg. (¼ tablet). Usually the people who have strong reactions to the side effects also have strong reactions to the drug itself and do not need the larger dosage.

Another major source of resistance to the use of Antabuse occurs in men and seems to stem from sexism. Men more often resist taking Antabuse than women. Men—more than women—feel that it is embarrassing and shameful not to be able to control their drinking without any help. The macho attitude that requires men to feel strong causes them to want to stop drinking without any help—especially the help of Antabuse. I sympathize with this attitude—it is hard to face up to lack of control—and I will always respond in an understanding manner to this wish. But I will also explain that a person need not be ashamed of needing help, and that the best way to work on problems of this sort is by using as much help from as many sources as possible. I also explain how sex-role scripting forces men to go it alone, without help, and how it is important to reject those expectations to profit from group therapy. But if an alcoholic *insists* that he wants to try to stop drinking without Antabuse, I would avoid arguing and would steer clear of the persecutory stance implied. I try to come up with a cooperative, negotiated agreement: if sobriety cannot be achieved without the

Antabuse within a reasonable period of time, I will insist that Antabuse be taken.

This discussion may seem puzzling or even ridiculous to some therapists who may say to themselves, "Why, this approach is based on having an alcoholic who is willing to stop drinking. But the very nature of alcoholism is that the person cannot or does not want to stop drinking. This approach is limited to people who are willing to stop drinking and who therefore are not really problems. It wouldn't work with somebody who is a real alcoholic. This approach is of limited value and doesn't deal with the real problem of alcoholism."

Of course, nobody who doesn't want to stop being an alcoholic will stop being an alcoholic. But there are many alcoholics who would like to and simply do not believe that they can. They have tried and failed. They have had violent withdrawal symptoms, they have given up over and over, and they have gone back to Devil Alcohol. They know that alcohol is destroying them, but they have developed a fatalistic, defeated attitude. This attitude may include arguments defending their right to drink on occasion or arguments minimizing the severity of their problem. But these are rationalizations which easily give way under the pressure of loving theraputic confrontation.

This approach brings to the surface the alcoholic's desire to stop drinking if it exists, and it exists in the great majority of alcoholics. I would never attempt to treat the minority of alcoholics who truly do not want to stop drinking. There seems to be no approach at this time that is effective with that group.

The Reluctant Quitter

Many alcoholics who are willing to stop drinking find that it is not possible to do so entirely and immediately.

Most people who come for help will stop drinking completely within a month or two of attending therapy sessions. There is always a smaller group who agree to the contract but do not stop drinking, and they fall into two categories.

One group continues to drink more or less continuously and attends meetings under the influence of alcohol. The other group reduces its drinking input and confines it to weekends or between sessions; they are sober during group meetings but drink in between.

The client who continues to drink steadily and attends therapy sessions under the influence of alcohol should be told that it is impossible to do psychotherapy under those conditions. Still, I always insist that he attend whether drunk or sober; and when he does, I make it a point to be friendly and nurturing, to ask how he feels, what his week has been like, and the extent and quantity of his drinking during the week. I will encourage him to speak about how he feels, since a person who is drunk is often in touch with emotions that are hidden when he is sober. This material can become important information for future therapy. I do not engage in lengthy discussions dealing with the reasons for drinking or any of the debates that alcoholics are fond of getting into—especially when they are drunk. I make sure that the inebriated client does not monopolize the session or take more than his fair share of time, and limit myself to being friendly, nurturing, concerned, and firmly insistent that the client come to group *sober* next time. I refuse to do Adult, "rational" work with a drunk alcoholic because it won't have any lasting effect. His Adult is out of commission. I do, however, try to convey a message of empathy and support which *will* penetrate that alcoholic fog and make an impression on his Child.

The alcoholic who drinks between meetings presents a different problem, since he drinks and keeps the therapist in the dark about it. This type of alcoholic usually plays D&P and puts the therapist in the role of the Victim/Patsy. By concealing the facts of his drinking, he finds out whether the therapist is experienced enough to pursue the matter and confront him. The therapist who doesn't will probably be completely ineffective.

While working with an alcoholic who is still drinking, the therapist should make sure that she remains aware of the quantity and extent of the drinking. This is accomplished by uninhibited questioning and by being open to whatever information may be volunteered by employers, friends, and relatives. Because awareness is the best defense against becoming a Victim/Patsy, employers, friends, and family are encouraged to communicate with the therapist. This is done openly, with the understanding that information will not be divulged without the alcoholic's permission. In this manner, confidence is preserved while awareness is maximized. Many therapists treat their client's relatives with aloofness verging on contempt. This attitude is usually rationalized as necessary to preserve confidentiality and trust, but it is really persecutory and wholly unnecessary. Instead, it is best to accept information as offered with the proviso that it must be evaluated and used with caution.

When the therapist refuses to play Victim/Patsy and continues to focus on the client's drinking he plays the antithesis to the Alcoholic game and thereby makes it possible for the alcoholic to choose an alternative to game playing. Eventually the alcoholic will either cease drinking entirely within three months or will frankly admit that she is not interested in changing her drinking behavior and will discontinue treatment. To date, a very small minority (approximately 10 percent) of alcoholics who have joined one of my groups realize that they don't want to quit drinking; they openly say so and discontinue treatment.

The Newly Abstaining Alcoholic

Once an alcoholic has stopped drinking, treatment takes a dramatic turn; until then all efforts are addressed primarily to the problem of helping him to stop. The first consequence of completely stopping drinking is a profound change in the quality of the person's consciousness. This can be the source of great alarm, and in most cases makes the person very uncomfortable. This *withdrawal panic* is particularly pronounced in people who have had a long history of uninterrupted drinking. People who have been on a steady diet of alcohol for many years and who suddenly stop drinking altogether are likely to report very disconcerting changes of consciousness in the second or third weeks of sobriety.

Withdrawal panic should be distinguished from *withdrawal sickness*. Both of these crises result from alcohol withdrawal, but the withdrawal sickness is mostly physiological: a real medical condition (especially in the extreme case of delirium tremens or D.T.'s, which is potentially fatal and may require hospitalization).

The withdrawal panic comes weeks later; and while it may have a subtle physical basis, it is primarily a psychological phenomenon.

Withdrawal panic may occur with or without withdrawal sickness. The pattern is usually: (1) Withdrawal sickness (if any) lasting not more than a week, followed by (2) a lull lasting about two weeks—sometimes less—during which the Parent ego state is dominant and during which the alcoholic feels very strong and confident. This is the well-known period when the alcoholic is "on the wagon" and feeling "on top of the world." This is followed by (3) withdrawal panic (if any) in which the alcoholic's Adapted Child becomes scared and anxious about the mental changes that result from the continued lack of alcohol in her system.

Not all persons who stop drinking undergo a severe withdrawal panic. People who do—and who are not on Antabuse—are likely to drink at this time. If they do not drink, they may become obsessed by thoughts of drinking and constantly struggle against these thoughts. When this struggle completely floods consciousness, the subtle mental changes which result from an alcohol-free nervous system are not as obvious as when the person is taking Antabuse.

People who take Antabuse are usually free of the desire to drink. Because they are not preoccupied with this struggle to avoid drinking, they become aware of the change caused by the absence of alcohol in their bodies. One patient reported waking up in the middle of the night with uncontrolled thoughts racing through his mind which somehow threatened to cause a mental explosion or breakdown similar to a short circuit in a computer. He felt extremely aware of minute bits of his wife's behavior, or of having insights into motives, conversations, or of seeing things such as trees and flowers in an alarmingly sharp and vivid way. Because of their newness and unfamiliarity all of these symptoms created great anxiety. He interpreted them in malignant terms; he felt as if he were about to lose his mind.

Some therapists interpret these reactions as evidence that alcoholism is a defense against the breakthrough of an "underlying psychosis." The theory that alcoholism often serves to protect the alcoholic from a preexisting psychosis is based on the observation that some alcoholics exhibit "psychotic symptoms," such as auditory hallucinations or paranoid states even after the withdrawal sickness is over. Another argument bolstering the theory: some alcoholics are able to maintain sobriety with the help of phenothiazines, which are known as "antipsychotic" drugs. These alcoholics are thus thought to be basically psychotic and only incidentally alcoholic. This determination may have several outcomes. The patient may be henceforth ignored as incurable, maintained on drugs, but otherwise ignored; or he may even be "allowed" to go back to drinking, since, it is argued, alcoholism is the lesser of the two evils.

I believe that any diagnosis of an underlying psychosis is not to be made lightly. I always assume that such symptoms are temporary and will subside, usually within one month. This was the case with the person described earlier and for many others who have gone through similar symptoms. The vast majority of patients who go through symptoms of this sort are in the grip of a withdrawal panic and are certainly not psychotic. They are experiencing an alcohol-free state which is so unfamiliar that it is frightening and difficult to comprehend.

For instance, from the point of view of his script, a man who stops drinking is going against the parental injunction that he not use his Adult, and that he not think. While he is drinking, he is in a Child ego state, which is going along with the injunctions of his Parent. The withdrawal sickness and consequent feeling of well-being are a period in which the Parent ego state runs the show and during which the Child willingly stays out of the picture. Withdrawal panic represents a gradual return of the fully functioning Adult ego state. This clear-thinking state of mind is unfamiliar and is a frightening development. It is a mode of functioning which was strongly enjoined against and disapproved of by the alcoholic's parents. He may never have experienced it until now. At this point the patient needs protection and strong reassurances that he is not crazy. He is experiencing an Adult ego state free of alcohol; within a few weeks, he will become accustomed to it and will be able to assimilate this new view of his world. Such reassurances are usually quite effective in countering the panic. At this point minor tranquilizers can help the patient deal with his feelings, but this dulls full awareness of the unencumbered Adult ego state and covertly reinforces the Parental injunction against Adult thought. Because of this, the use of medication is strongly discouraged unless it is absolutely necessary. Instead, in addition to reassurance, soothing teas, hot baths, massages, and other relaxing activities are recommended.

Additional symptoms observed during the withdrawal panic are dizziness, loss of balance, insomnia, mental anguish, nightmares, extreme cold, extreme hunger, blurred vision, and feelings of being clairvoyant or telepathic. Whether these symptoms are low-level remains of withdrawal sickness or whether they are purely psychological in nature is unclear. They are reasonable sequels to withdrawal from long-term alcohol abuse, not a sign of psychosis.

Following this period of panic (if the patient does not escape from it into renewed drinking), there is usually a "honeymoon," in which the patient becomes accustomed to the drug-free Adult ego state and during which he feels genuine relief and well-being. The "honeymoon" tends to include freedom from games and intense script behavior, and may last as long as three months. However, it can be expected to subside; and even though the patient may remain sober, the games which are linked to his specific game of Alcoholic and his script—whatever it is—will begin to manifest themselves in a new, more moderate, nondrinking context.

Everyone who has been an alcoholic and has stopped drinking will be faced (as is anyone who gives up a major game) with an existential vacuum relating to the many hours each day that need to be structured and which cannot be structured as they were when they were drinking. Many alcoholics who stop drinking attempt to continue structuring time in familiar ways by going to a bar after work. Other people, who are aware of the difficulties of attempting to structure time in old ways, will find themselves completely at a loss and unable to find satisfactory new methods. A therapist who proposes to help these people must aid them in finding ways to structure time as part of their homework.

For one patient, a schedule of activities was constructed to cover every waking hour of the day for a whole week. Another patient who was very shy and reluctant to contact friends made several calls during the group meeting to arrange various activities and dates. Many alcoholics find that when they stop drinking and choose to remove themselves from their alcoholic circle, they become solitary and lose the few sources of strokes that they had when they were drinking. The depression resulting from this loss of strokes is a very common problem at this point.

For married people with children, there is usually an increased positive interaction corresponding with the "honeymoon" period after withdrawal. This eventually yields to a period in which it seems that the members of the family not only expect—but almost seem to wish—that the alcoholic would resume drinking. This phenomenon is easily understood when we remember that alcoholism is a game that requires *several* players. The wife and children of the alcoholic are usually full participants in the game and feel a vacuum in their lives when the alcoholic stops drinking similar to what is felt by the alcoholic himself. Thus, the alcoholic in a family might feel an even stronger urge to drink than a person who can leave his "game" social circle behind. In addition to his own internal compulsion to drink, he will feel the pressures applied by his family.

Because the healing of a married alcoholic requires changes in two or more people, it almost seems at times that the single alcoholic has a better prognosis. The very real difficulty which is added for the alcoholic by the presence of a family is usually overshadowed by the positive influence that families are able to provide. I have sometimes thought that a certain alcoholic might profit by a separation or divorce from her spouse because of the difficulties mentioned above, only to find that, if the problems are worked through, the family is a great adjunct to the person's health as a source of strokes and as a basis for existential meaning. Sometimes, however, the family really pushes the alcoholic to return to drinking and a cure may require a separation between the two partners.

People who achieve sobriety by taking Antabuse generally want to stop taking it within six months. This desire should be regarded with suspicion. After six months of sobriety without a desire to drink, most people feel that it should no longer be necessary to take Antabuse. They yearn for the feelings of autonomy and self-determination that are implicit in not having to rely on the drug. However, as soon as Antabuse is discontinued, alcoholics will almost always begin to think about drinking, which may start them drinking again. It has been my experience that every alcoholic drinks again after some months of sobriety. In the context of ongoing group therapy, this episode need not be disastrous, but may actually refresh the patient's memory about the realities of drinking. Except for the alcoholic who goes on an extremely self-destructive binge, one or perhaps two such relapses can have some positive educational aspects. The nature and extent of the drinking episode is usually a good indication of whether the therapy is having any effect.

Generally, these episodes are shorter and less severe than the previous episodes, and this represents improvement in Adult control. A binge which is as bad or worse than previous ones indicates that therapy has not been effective and that the patient is only making superficial "progress" with no real changes in Adult control. People who are improving will emerge from the episode considerably wiser; they will have had a chance to review the different aspect of their drinking in a situation of improved Adult awareness and control, an experience that invariably proves to be sobering. However, for effective healing a full year of sobriety needs to follow.

Discontinuing Antabuse, as well as having the first "social" drink after a long period of sobriety, is regarded by most people as a public declaration that the person is now O.K. Because it flies in the face of his Enemy (who says he is not-O.K.) as well as many recovered alcoholics and of A.A. (who say it isn't possible), these events are always potential trouble spots. The therapist has to treat such landmarks with finesse, since he is neither a Patsy who blindly accepts drinking as a harmless act, nor a Persecutor who predicts certain doom. The best attitude is the Adult wait-and-see, backed up by a promise of Protection no matter what happens.

The Counterscript

As we know, people operate under the compulsion of scripts. Alcoholism as a script compels the alcoholic to uncontrollable drinking and self-damaging behavior. But there always are periods in the life of the alcoholic when she is not drinking or being self-destructive.

These periods are interesting because they frequently appear to be permanent cures of the problem in the eyes of the alcoholic and his circle. Between alcoholic bouts no one really knows whether the person has really changed into a nonalcoholic. Only time can tell whether the script is just dormant, waiting to re-emerge in full bloom, or whether it has been abandoned.

The counterscript is that part of the script in which the person is temporarily not following the most obviously damaging requirements of the script. During this period, the alcoholic is sober, content, and productive, but has not given up the script, which will return inevitably.

A.A.'s point of view maintains that the alcoholic can never give up the script and that any periods of sobriety are merely a temporary counterscript. But my observations of alcoholics indicate that people who were once excessive drinkers differ. Some people give up the script; some are merely in a counterscript phase of the alcoholic script.

The most convincing change for an alcoholic is a protracted period of moderate social drinking. However, since many cured alcoholics lose interest in alcohol, this criterion is not always available. In general, the loss of preoccupation with alcohol—either the alcoholic pastimes, or the game in any of its roles—is a good criterion. A radical change in time structuring and the development of avenues of enjoyment without alcohol are crucial indicators of a script change. In addition, an often subtle change in the physical appearance of the alcoholic is a reliable index though difficult to assess. The alcoholic in a counterscript is tense, anxious, "up-tight," even when smiling and enjoying himself, as if constantly on the brink of relaxing and letting go, which he feels he can't do for fear that his "script will take over. The former alcoholic lacks this "on the brink" quality and therefore looks and "feels" quite different from the alcoholic in a counterscript.

However, I must warn the reader not to take this section too seriously—especially if it means that he or she is going to use the information to try to diagnose any one person's sobriety as being a "real" script change or merely a temporary counterscript. That type of analysis of other people's lives is presumptuous and meddlesome. Aside from the fact that it can lead to the wrong diagnosis, it is also of very little use. This is why I mention it only as an afterthought. Sobriety is the first step for an alcoholic and it is clear that it is hardly ever enough. Many changes have to follow sobriety for alcoholism to be completely cured. These changes are what we are interested in; whether a person is *really* cured is nobody's business but his own. Only he can answer the question, and then only to himself.

15

How to Help
Without Rescuing

People often ask me, "What is the secret of good psychotherapy?" According to my mood, my answer often is, "One-third not Rescuing, One-third Transactional Analysis and Radical Psychiatry, and one-third hasn't been figured out yet."

You don't have to be a trained psychotherapist to help an alcoholic because so much of what can be done is simply a matter of not Rescuing, or, in other words, not playing the game. I believe everyone who reads these lines has had the experience of Rescuing someone else. We all know that gut-wrenching feeling of being sucked deeper and deeper into doing more and more with and for a deeply troubled person who seems to be getting nowhere fast. Each renewed effort starts with hope and ends in disappointment. Yet it seems that not helping would be heartless and selfish.

Or we may have experienced the anger and dismay of seeing months of support and involvement in seeming success dissolve into a binge or a similar breakdown. These are traumatic experiences for the Rescuer; but, as I have said repeatedly, they are also harmful to the Victim and they must be avoided for the sake of everyone involved.

As I have said before, Rescuing is simply a matter of:

(1) Doing more than your share of the work in a relationship, and/or

(2) Doing something you don't want to do.

Doing One's Share

How do you know when you are doing more than your share in helping another person? This is not always clear. In an attempt to develop Rescue-free relationships, some people have carried this concept to extremes. Rescuing has been misunderstood by some to mean being distant and noncommittal, avoiding a warm, nurturing attitude with anyone who needs help. This is not what I mean; when not Rescuing is carried to that extreme, it is a subtle form of persecution. Doing your share in a relationship is a much more subtle process than merely staying aloof. Consider the following telephone conversation I once had with a man who eventually joined one of my groups:

C.S.: Hello.

Mr. A. (Surprised at hearing a male voice rather than an answering-service operator): Hello . . . May I speak with Dr. Steiner?

C.S: This *is* Dr. Steiner.

Mr. A. (Seems disappointed): Oh, I didn't expect to get you on the phone.

C.S: Well, here I am.

Mr. A. (Somewhat hesitant): I'm calling because my sister thought I should speak to you.

C.S: About what?

Mr. A.: Well, she says I'm an alcoholic.

C.S (Cheerfully): Well, good, thanks for calling. What do *you* say?

Mr. A. (Startled): About what?

C.S: About being an alcoholic.

Mr. A.: Well, to be perfectly honest, I'm not sure I know. I guess I am an alcoholic.

C.S: Okay. What can I do for you?

Mr. A.: Well, I really don't know.

C.S. (Nicely): I'm sure I don't know if *you* don't know. Why don't you call me back when you know what you want from me? I'm usually easy to reach, and you can—

Mr. A. (Anxious): She said that you have classes for alcoholics.

C.S: That's right. Actually, they're not classes, they are therapy sessions.

Mr. A.: I guess I should come to one of the sessions.

C.S: What for?

Mr. A.: Well, to try 'em.

C.S: That would be okay, but I don't think you really want to come ... (Silence—no reaction from Mr. A.) Why don't you tell your sister that you spoke to me and tell her that we agreed that it probably wouldn't work. That way she will be satisfied, and I will be able to go back to what I was doing before you called.

Mr. A. (Relieved): You don't think it would work? Why not?

C.S: Well, because you really don't want to do it, and therapy never works for people who don't want it.

Mr. A.: I can see that, and I really don't want to do it right now.

C.S: Well, if you don't want to do it, I don't want to do it either. Thank you for calling. You didn't tell me your name.

Mr. A.: The name is Ambig. Carl Ambig.

C.S: Okay, Mr. Ambig, nice talking to you.

Mr. A.: Well, maybe I *should* try it.

C.S: I'll tell you what. I think you should think about it. I'm always here—you don't have to decide right now. I have group therapy once a week, and if you want to know more about it, you can read my book *Healing Alcoholism*, or you can call me again. Okay?

Mr. A.: Okay. Good-bye.

C.S: Bye.

Sometimes, visualizing my interactions with clients reminds me of a dance I often go through with Suzie, a very wily horse. Sometimes Suzie does not want to be ridden; and when she sees me approaching, with an apple in my hand, I can see that she wants to come closer, but at the same time does not trust me not to capture her. I hold out the apple. She looks at me, pricks up her ears, and moves in my direction cautiously. If I become too eager and start walking in her direction, she stops and slowly starts turning around. If I stop, she stops. If I now turn around and start walking away, she whinnies and starts moving after me. Once again, I turn around and offer her the apple. She comes closer. Eventually, we meet at some imaginary middle point and she takes the apple. The feeling is one of increasing involvement and trust as she cautiously assesses the situation until she decides to move in closer and trust me.

I have a lot of respect for people who, knowing nothing about me, approach me with great caution. After all, I am a shrink, and shrinks deserve to be distrusted. There are many psychotherapists whose practices are reasonably full who want nothing to do with alcoholics and who would treat them unkindly. There are also many psychotherapists whose practices are failing and who will take on anybody who can help pay the bills, regardless of whether they know anything about the problem. I'm sure that Mr. A. has been offered a great deal of help which hasn't turned out to be very helpful. And I have sympathy for his doubts that the therapy I offer will help him at all. I can see that he is under pressure from his sister to make some kind of move, and that he would be willing to go through the motions of attending a few group sessions until she was mollified. I can see also that he is intrigued by my approach. I was doing something that I wanted to go back to when the phone rang, and I didn't want to spend a lot of time beating around the bush. I certainly didn't need to start any Rescues. My transactions are attempts at showing some interest without going too far over the line, to "neither a Patsy nor a Rescuer be."

Here it helps to see human interaction in terms of transactions and to be able to do a transactional analysis of important interactions. As we have seen, a transaction is made up of a stimulus and a response. Many initial therapy conversations are like a fishing trip. "Bait and nibble" or "bait and hook" or "bait, nibble, and run." One person sets the bait and the other responds by nibbling, biting, or running. In this conversation we are both fishing. He is fishing for an out from his sister's pressure, and I am fishing for some real interest. We are both in danger of biting and swallowing a Rescue.

However, while I am not biting, I am also not running. I am trying to be friendly and cheerful even though it is obvious that Mr. A. is not really interested—at first. I don't fall for the hooks, but I also don't run from the interaction.

In our everyday interactions, we are often offered a baited hook which would involve us in a Rescue if we bit. While this is true, there is no point in being paranoid about it. Knowing what constitutes a Rescue and learning to say no when we realize we are in one is not all that difficult. It is possible, then, to relax and be a friendly and neighborly person without danger of becoming a Patsy.

With Mr. A.'s example, I have tried to illustrate the process of talking with one who needs help, without Rescuing. When working in a group it helps to visualize the situation between the people involved in terms of a space between them. Two or more people are sitting around an initially empty space. As the conversation proceeds, everyone puts something into that space. The people in the helping role, whether they be therapist, friends, or group members, ask questions, put in suggestions, or offer nurturing. The person who has taken the role of being helped (let's call him Carl again) examines the offerings and chooses what he wants. If he likes a suggestion or accepts a criticism, he picks it up and acts on it. If he doesn't, he leaves it alone.

If Carl wants the nurturing he is offered, he accepts it. The helpers are keenly aware of Carl and what he takes and what he rejects. If he is eager, then the helpers become eager as well. If he is reluctant, the helpers sit back; the helpers and Carl maintain a balance of activity. If Carl rejects a number of ideas, then the helpers stop making suggestions. I have a personal rule that I call "Three strikes and you're out!" in which I keep track of the suggestions I make. When three of them are rejected for any reason at all, I stop. I may even say, out loud, "Strike Three." I might explain that I've made three suggestions that must not have been very good and have therefore struck out. This may sound facetious, but it really isn't, because I truly believe that any suggestion that is rejected probably was not a good one. It was either not put in the proper words, so the person could understand it, or it was poorly timed, or perhaps—wonder of wonders—it was really a poor suggestion. I am of the opinion that a valid, properly worded and timed suggestion will be accepted, and that when a suggestion is rejected, there was probably something wrong with it.

Not Rescuing helps because it rejects the Victim role. To the alcoholic's plea, "Help me, I can't do it," the response of the effective helper is, "I am interested in helping you if I can see what you are doing on your own behalf. What *are* you doing for yourself? What else can you do? What will you do if I help you? What would you like *me* to do? Let's make a deal—I'll do X if you do Y. If I change my mind, I'll let you know."

It is also necessary to be able to say, "I understand that you would like me to help you, but I don't feel I have the desire (or time) (or energy)."

Not Rescuing additionally avoids Persecution. Persecution is the inevitable result of Rescues, and for every minute that a person spends Rescuing another, it is inevitable that another minute will be spent Persecuting. Yet, since no one is perfect, and no one can really avoid Rescues every once in a while (as I keep noticing myself), it is important to know how to deal with one's Persecution tendencies as well as one's Rescue tendencies. First, it is important to recognize that Persecution is a harmful transaction and that when we feel angry at others because they're not working hard, or because they're rejecting all of our moves, or because they are not getting better, that this anger is our responsibility and should not be foisted on them. When, for one reason or another, after having Rescued, a feeling of persecution emerges, it is important to say so and to take the responsibility for it.

"Carl, I am getting angry at you because you are not accepting my suggestions (or because what I do doesn't seem to help). I realize that I shouldn't be angry and that my anger has to do with trying too hard. I apologize for having Rescued you and I will try not to be angry. I hope you will understand if I pull back a bit and stop trying so hard."

Having spoken so strongly against Rescues, I feel I need to say a few words to prevent too strong a reaction in the opposite direction. I call this reaction an anti-Rescue and believe it to be a subtle form of Persecution in which our present fear of helping is a reaction to mistakes of the past. An effective therapist is willing to stick her neck out a little to start the ball rolling. Being initially eager, helpful, friendly, and active does not mean that one is Rescuing.

One other assumption is that to simply nurture someone who is hurt or feels powerless or in distress is a Rescue. I think it is very important to distinguish between a Rescue and nurturing. When someone is upset and is showing his feelings freely, I see it as a very substantial contribution toward improvement. I feel no qualms about responding with some feelings of my own. Most of the times when a person cries, the tears are a genuine expression of feelings of despair and powerlessness. People's anger reflects their frustration. I will assume that these are honest feelings and will respond in kind. Only if this becomes a pattern, where the person gets angry or cries or engages in emotional outbursts repeatedly, without any visible change, will I then assume and consider the possibility that I should not respond lovingly and that perhaps, as some T.A. therapists say, "I am stroking a racket."

Nurturing someone is not automatically a Rescue; it is a legitimate aspect of helping people. Not nurturing someone who is genuinely upset is, once again, a subtle form of Persecution. Some people who become therapists and who have problems being loving and nurturing will use the concept of Rescue to justify their lack of warmth, but this use of the concept is an easy cop-out and nothing more.

Ten Rules to Avoid Rescues

Although there are many ways of Rescuing an alcoholic, some ways are typical. Here are ten of them:

1. When three or more suggestions to an alcoholic have been rejected, you are Rescuing. Instead, offer one or two, and wait to see whether they are acceptable. If they are not, stop making suggestions. Don't play "Why don't you . . . Yes, but . . ."

2. It's O.K. to investigate possible therapists for an alcoholic, but never make an appointment for him or her. Any therapist who is willing to make an appointment with an alcoholic through a third person is probably a potential Rescuer and eventual Persecutor.

3. Do not remove liquor, pour liquor down the drain, or look for hidden stashes of liquor in an alcoholic's house, unless you're asked to do so by the alcoholic. Conversely, do not ever buy, serve, mix for, or offer alcohol to an alcoholic.

4. Do not engage in lengthy conversations about alcoholism or a person's alcoholic problem while the person is drunk or drinking; that will be a waste of time and energy, and will be completely forgotten by him in most cases.

5. Never lend money to a drinking alcoholic. Do not allow a drunk alcoholic to come to your house, or, worse, drink in your

house. Instead, in as loving and nurturing a way as possible, ask to see her again when she is sober.

6. Do not get involved in errands, repair jobs, cleanups, long drives, pickups, or deliveries for an alcoholic who is not actively participating in fighting his alcoholism.

7. When you are relating to an alcoholic, do not commit the common error of seeing only the good and justifying the bad. "He's so wonderful when he's not drunk" is a common mistake people make with respect to alcoholics. The alcoholic is a whole person, and his personality includes both his good part and his bad part. They cannot be separated from each other. Either take the whole person or none at all. If the ledger comes out consistently in the red, it is foolish to look only on the credit side.

8. Do not remain silent on the subject of another's alcoholism. Don't hesitate to express yourself freely on the subject: what you don't like, what you won't stand for, what you think about it, what you want or how it makes you feel. But don't do it with the expectation of creating a change—do it just to be on record. Often your outspoken attitude will be taken seriously and appreciated, though it may not bring about any immediate changes.

9. Be aware of doing anything that you don't want to do for the alcoholic. It is bad enough if you commit any of the above mistakes willingly. But when you add to them the complications of doing them when you would prefer not to, you are compounding your mistake and fostering an eventual persecution.

10. Never believe that an alcoholic is hopeless. Keep your willingness to help ready, offer it often, and make it available whenever you detect a genuine interest and effort on the alcoholic's part. When that happens, don't overreact, but help cautiously and without Rescuing, doing only what you want to do, and no more than your share.

Remembering these guidelines about Rescuing will be helpful regardless of what else is done.

Let us now look at what can be done specifically for the alcoholic, other than not Rescuing.

16

The Enemy

Working with the alcoholic script implies helping people to get rid of the injunctions, attributions, and destructive internal dialogues that originate within them, in their Enemy. This chapter is a practical guide to fighting the Enemy. It is written with the alcoholic in mind but to some extent it applies to everyone: we all take on internalized oppressive messages in the process of growing up.

The Enemy is a reality in everyone's life. However, the extent to which this reality is perceived and understood by people varies greatly from person to person. The Enemy can be, in one person's awareness, simply a dark, evil influence, settling over the mind like a suffocating blanket which turns everything dismal, without warning. To another person, it is a nagging, insistent voice. It can appear as a rational-sounding, sedate, moderate, occasional statement which undercuts every important effort. The Enemy can operate in the form of nightmares, physical aches and pains, or white-hot flashes of dread.

No matter what particular form the Enemy takes, it is essential to its survival and effectiveness that it not be challenged by the victim of its abuse. The Enemy continues to operate because the person is willing to countenance it and to accept it as a valid part of the world. The recognition that it is an arbitrary set of messages that has been internalized and is now being listened to is crucial. As long as it is listened to, believed, and followed, the Enemy has power. To eliminate the Enemy's power it is essential that several steps are consecutively followed:

First: locate the Enemy. Where is it? What form does it take?

What feelings does it prey on? Guilt? Shame? Fear? Low self-esteem?

Second: how does the person remove his support of the Enemy so that it loses its potency and returns to its external form: an oppressive influence, which needs to be watched and struggled against.

Third: what specific techniques are effective to counteract the Enemy's influence?

The three steps outlined above will be explored below.

Stalking the Enemy

The process of making the Enemy conscious and demystifying the way it operates is analogous to peeling an onion. Its messages are layered; as we become aware of and begin to discard one layer, another layer comes into view. Some people begin work on a totally unpeeled onion, while others have already discarded a number of layers. In any case, starting from the most mystified Enemy, I will describe several layers that a person might have to work through.

The first and most obscure layer of the Enemy can be merely a negative emotion of some sort. The emotion can be a very subtle feeling of impending doom or it can be a sudden fright. It can be a persistent hatred, a creeping doubt, a dread of death or disease, free-floating anxiety or a claustrophobic feeling. The experience is often one that does not seem to be attached to anything in particular. The person learns that the feeling can engulf her anytime. Often, whenever the person is feeling good, the fear that a negative emotion will make its appearance is usually an omen that brings on the Enemy. "Things are going too well—it must end soon." "Whenever I feel this good I inevitably feel bad later." An alcoholic might suddenly realize that he's had a whole week of careless, happy days without a single thought about drinking and will suddenly be overcome with anxiety. This is merely the first stage of the Enemy's blitz. The next stage of the attack is the familiar feeling of fear, dread, doubt, which is the specific favorite of that person's Enemy, and which in the alcoholic's mind can be dealt with only by drinking. Each Enemy has its own specific messages and its own specific techniques. In fact, each Enemy is just like a complex, real person, with strengths and weaknesses, tricks, and strategies of its own.

An Enemy attack can last for a few intense seconds and spoil a person's day, or it can start slowly and build up to a fierce pitch, which then subsides. A strong desire to drink can take a minute, a day, a week, or even longer, depending on the Enemy's power. One of the most familiar and feared experiences for alcoholics are those periods of time during which strong negative emotions combined with a strong desire to drink completely invade their consciousness.

It is important that the person learn to recognize the specific feeling that is characteristic of his Enemy. After having identified the feeling, the next step is to recognize that there is always a cause for its onset. This cause may be a verbal statement, or an image, or a series of images. There is always some sort of mental activity that accompanies the feelings.

The movie: One person had sudden attacks of anxiety that came from nowhere, as far as she could tell. After focusing on the mental events surrounding the attack, she realized that they were always preceded by a wordless fantasy, a sort of private silent movie of the mind. It was merely an image of her standing in front of a large crowd of people who were jeering, pointing at her, laughing, and throwing stones as she stood terrified, wondering what she had done.

Another man's Enemy approached him through a sudden fear of death which was simply a feeling of lying in a coffin with his eyes closed and being led somewhere, probably to his grave. Other pre-verbal Enemy attacks can be fantasies of being killed, raped, of failing miserably, starving to death, being hated by everyone around, being tortured, or getting cancer or some other dread disease. For alcoholics, sooner or later, these fantasies become attached reflexively to the desire to drink. This happens because alcohol has a very strong sedating effect which tends to wipe out such strong negative emotions. A conditioned reflex develops: anxiety brings on a desire to drink in the same way that the proverbial bell brought on salivation in Pavlov's dogs.

The first defense against such an attack is to make that pre-conscious "movie" clearly conscious: to discover its contents and to become aware every time that it intrudes into one's consciousness.

This can only be done with a clear mind, free of drugs. Any chemical that affects thinking will interfere with this and any of the steps necessary.

The score: Having discovered the fantasy which comes with the attack, the next step in stalking the Enemy is to find the verbal content or "score" which goes along with the movie. It is always possible to find the verbal messages behind the attack. The words that are attached to the fantasy might be: "You are going to die," or "Everybody hates you," or "You'll get a heart attack," or "You'll never succeed," or "You are rotten and no good," or "Have a drink—it's the only way to feel better," or "It's hopeless—you might as well give up and get drunk." These may be heard as clear, loud voices, or as ominous whispers. One woman saw them written under a picture of herself drunk and alone.

During the next stage of the battle, it helps to get a small notebook to keep an "attack diary." Each attack or bad feeling— even if the person isn't sure of its source—is recorded, with the fantasy and verbal content behind it whenever possible. This way the person starts to become conscious of the actual dimensions of the Enemy's offensives. Some people find that when the Enemy strikes, it totally blanks out every other mental activity for seconds, minutes, or hours. Some people feel completely overwhelmed and others only feel a slight annoyance. In any case, documentation of the Enemy's activity and exact messages is important.

People who are quite willing to keep a record of their negative feelings may or may not be willing to accept that these experiences represent Enemy attacks: that they are false ideas, introduced into consciousness by an external source of the past which has now been internalized. People have a tendency to be willing to assume that the predictions and statements of the Enemy should be considered valid. "I *may* get cancer. All the people in my family have . . ." Or "I *may* fail—I have failed all my life so far." Or "I *am* no good. I have ruined three marriages, and my children are all in trouble." Or "I *am* stupid. I can't even balance my checkbook." Or "There *is* no hope—I might as well get drunk." These are all examples of the way in which people will actually take sides with their Enemy and defend its point of view. This brings us to the second stage in the battle: making conscious the external origin of the Enemy.

Separating the Self from the Enemy

When the fantasy and the words associated with the Enemy are located, it is essential to reemphasize the external source of *all* the negative messages. The most difficult part of the struggle is making clear that the Enemy is *always* wrong.

In order to succeed, it is necessary to differentiate between Enemy messages and Adult messages which may be critical in content. The critical messages coming from the Adult, such as "If you do it this way it won't work." Or "There is a good chance that you will not get this job." Or "If you continue to smoke, you are likely to get cancer," are not really negative messages about ourselves; they are statements of probabilities. Even though they are associated with negative outcomes, they are not Enemy messages. Enemy messages attack people with not-O.K. putdowns.

If we assume that every human being is O.K., beautiful, smart, health-seeking and good, then we can also assume that any statement to the contrary ("You are not-O.K." "She is bad, stupid, ugly, crazy, sick") is a falsehood. When a person tells himself such falsehoods, they need to be rejected. We must choose between whether we are basically O.K. or not. The choice between these two views is really a matter of preference, but I believe that we are basically positive beings. True, at times it seems that we can see evidence for either point of view, but the recorded history of humankind shows a progressive—if faltering—climb away from destruction, theft, and murder, which reveals our positive bent.

In any case, our choice in Transactional Analysis and Radical Psychiatry is to embrace the view that people are basically good. This choice was put in words by Eric Berne when he said that the first and universal existential position held by people about people is "I'm O.K., You're O.K." Our view implies that the nasty, demeaning things we say about ourselves (and about other people) are falsehoods to be rejected.

One of the most effective ways of showing the basic falsehood of Enemy statements is that they are usually blatantly opportunistic. For example, one classic form of harassment is "You are a failure. You never do anything." One woman who was plagued by this type of statement also reported that whenever she succeeded in something, she would tell herself: "You are trying too hard—most people could do this with no effort at all." When I pointed out that she could not win no matter what she did, she said, "That's right! Come to think of it, when things come real easy, my Enemy says, 'That doesn't count—it was too easy.' "

The same opportunism shows itself in the rationalizations that are conjured up to justify the alcoholic's drinking. Whether happy, unhappy, upset, bored, alone, or in company, all situations are occasion for a drink.

Another favorite paradox the Enemy likes to use is illustrated by the following example: John reported extreme feelings of incompetence and stupidity, reinforced by constant voices in his head, saying, "You dumb bastard, you're retarded. How can you be so stupid?"

A group member commented, "That's your Enemy," and John answered, "I know—and I feel real stupid for having such a heavy Critical Parent."

During this phase, it is very hard for a person under the influence of the Enemy to see her separateness from it. For years she has taken the truth of these statements for granted. Moreover, there is no real evidence that the therapist can muster to disprove these statements. Everyone fails sooner or later. Everyone makes mistakes. Everyone commits occasional evil acts. So when a person hears, "You are evil," or "You are wrong," or "You'll never succeed," it is hard to see that this is an Enemy strategy, rather than a true statement. The therapist has to point out continually the difference between an objective, calm statement of negative expectation, ("You'll be late to work") or ("If you don't rest you'll get sick") or ("People will be angry if you don't stop") and an intense, accusatory, damning, emotional attack on the O.K.ness of the person, which is characteristic of the Enemy.

Sometimes people will hotly argue in defense of their own Enemy. It needs to be pointed out at this time that the person's insistence in maintaining and defending the Enemy position is in itself part of the Enemy's hold on his consciousness. In time, the therapist may need to point out that this is an unfair situation, one in which the therapist is trying to fight both the client and the client's Enemy.

This process can take weeks—sometimes months—to accomplish, and the therapist needs to be patient and should under no circumstances overextend herself to the point of irritation. She needs to simply point out repeatedly and whenever relevant that the client is having an Enemy attack and that he is again siding with his Enemy against himself.

It should be remembered that in a therapeutic contract which involves cooperation—and thus no Rescues—the therapist should never do more than half the work in the struggle. Therefore it is essential that the client do her part by actively fighting alongside the therapist. When the client sides with her Enemy, she is essentially embracing the Victim role. If the therapist indulges in a Rescue, he will eventually have to Persecute her. This process has to be engaged in slowly and patiently, always making sure that the client is equally involved and is taking equal responsibility in the struggle.

Once this particular portion of the work is completed—the emotional fantasy and verbal content (the movie and the score) of the Enemy as an external influence which can be separated from the self and fought effectively—we come to the third stage of the struggle: the development of the specific strategies that will defeat the Enemy.

Techniques

Exposure: One of the most effective techniques against the Enemy is exposing it to other people. As long as we harbor its ideas, they have power over our consciousness because they go unchallenged within our minds. In group therapy, with eight people listening, the act of stating openly what the Enemy says has a tremendously cleansing effect. It is as if the Enemy is a creature which can live only in the murky shadows of our minds. As we overturn the rocks under which the Enemy lives and open it up to the group's perceptions, it tends to shrink and die away almost by itself. Very often this approach is sufficient to defeat the Enemy; but in other cases, even when a person realizes what is going on, there will be continued attacks.

Confrontation: Each attack must be analyzed in detail, and specific confrontations must be developed. Some people will try to turn deaf ears to the Enemy's statements; some people will shout back; some people will argue logically. And while each one of these techniques might work with one Enemy, it may not work with another.

One Enemy may be a nagging, insistent presence which follows a person from room to room, constantly repeating its accusations. This is not one you can easily turn a deaf ear to. Instead, it might be more effective to face it squarely and say calmly, "Get out of here! If I ever see you again, I'm going to kill you!" That approach may not work with a brutal, bloodthirsty Enemy which can be defeated only by pumping oneself up to a large size and staring it down until it disappears.

Each Enemy has its particular source of power and it is necessary to match its power with power. The clever, devious, mind-raping Enemy needs an equally clever response; the one that predicts illness and death requires a radiant, healthy self-confidence; the one that lies deliberately requires truthfulness and knowledge of what is and isn't true.

Nurturing: The Nurturing Parent or Ally is the natural foe of the Enemy. When being attacked it is often very effective to get nurturing either from oneself or from another person.

In this connection, it is important to be able to distinguish Nurturing (You are O.K.) statements from Enemy (You are Not-O.K.) statements. Usually the difference is obvious:

Ally: I love you.
Enemy: I hate you.
Ally: You are beautiful.
Enemy: You are ugly.
Ally: Go on—you can do it.
Enemy: It'll never work.
Ally: Go ahead, enjoy yourself.
Enemy: You don't deserve it.

So far so good, but at times what appears to be a Nurturing statement is contaminated with Enemy ideas:

"You are very pretty for someone who is as fat as you."

"You are my favorite child." (Competitive—puts other children down.)

"I don't hate you." (Any negative word in the statement is suspected as being Enemy-originated.)

And even, given a certain tone, a sentence like "Go ahead,

enjoy yourself," can have an Enemy undercurrent because it might really be a rejection, rather than an encouragement.

One important form of contamination occurs when the Ally's statement is one of concern and nurturing which has as its core an assumption that the person is incompetent in some way. Often the nurturing of children has this aspect: it stifles the child's capacities to take care of itself. Specifically, in the case of eating habits, later transferred to alcoholic scripts, the parent encourages the child to eat, eat, eat so that it won't get sick. Unfortunately, this attitude assumes that the child cannot judge what food it needs and inter-feres with learning what, how, and when to eat. What seems benign and helpful Nurturing turns out to be Enemy contaminated.

The best way to decide whether a certain Nurturing statement is "clean" is to subject it to the scrutiny of the group. If no one in the group objects, it is probably "true-blue nurturing."

Asking for (and getting) or giving oneself nurturing strokes is a most potent antidote against the Enemy. Strokes can be written down and hung in a prominent place like the bedroom or kitchen where they can easily be seen at strategic times. Strokes can also be tape-recorded and kept near the bed or in the car to be played back when needed.

Whichever form the strokes take (from self or others, verbal, physical, written, spoken, or recorded) the person has to be alert to the moment they are needed most—during an Enemy attack.

How to Develop a Strong Ally

Like the Adult, the Nurturing ego state can be exercised and developed. We all have at least a small capacity for nurturing, but most of us do not have permission to nurture ourselves. Women are encouraged to be nurturing and therefore tend to have strong Allies, but their nurturing is reserved for men and children—not for themselves. Men, on the other hand, are discouraged from being nurturing because it is considered "women's work." Consequently, they tend to have underdeveloped Allies; because of their sexist training to be tough, men do not nurture themselves, or each other.

As a result, neither men nor women are able to be their own best friends or allies and do not take care of themselves in time of need. But the Enemy is given plenty of support for its work and usually functions unopposed. The answer is to strengthen the Ally.

Helping a person develop a strong Ally involves giving him permission to nurture and love himself. The person who wishes to learn nurturing behavior can observe other people's nurturing, copy it, and practice it whenever appropriate.

Being deliberately nurturing instead of rational, seeking out situations in which to Nurture without Rescuing, practicing taking care of, serving, or nursing others are different ways of strengthening the Ally. As the person learns nurturing behavior, she also needs to nurture herself, which is an additional, separate task. When nurturing themselves, people can expect strong interference from the Enemy, who will argue loudly: "You are being selfish and ridiculous." "First you have to take care of others." "This will never work." "The only thing that'll make you feel better is a drink. Go ahead, have one!"

A person may choose to develop a strong Ally as a contract in the group. This has proven very effective since it is very easy to practice nurturing in the group. The same can be done within a family or friendship circle; it works best if everyone is aware of the person's desire to become more nurturing and supports his effort.

Developing a strong Ally can take some time—often months— but it never fails to be a rewarding activity. Nurturing people (especially men) are much appreciated. Even more important, a strong Ally is the best weapon against the Enemy.

Avoiding Enemy Collusions

Insulating oneself from people whose Enemy colludes with or agrees with our own is another important technique. This often involves a separation from relatives who hold the same opinions which are the original source of our Enemy, or friends who were chosen in the past because they shared what later turned out to be Enemy points of view.

Relating to someone who shares our Enemy's opinions can lead to *collusions* in which two or more people develop blind spots for certain points of view which they hold. Scapegoating is an example of such a collusion. Racism and other forms of prejudice such as sexism are mass collusions. One common collusion of alcoholics is the feeling that private matters should not be discussed openly. One alcoholic once said to me, "I'd rather drink than think." This is a common attitude among alcoholics as is "I'd rather drink than talk about myself," and "I'd rather drink than work it out."

It is necessary to avoid such collusions to effectively fight the Enemy. This can be done by mutual agreements to be critical of each other's Enemy-originated statements and attitudes. However, sometimes other people aren't willing to make such deals, especially if they don't agree that the statements and opinions in question are objectionable. Then it may be necessary to avoid contact with those people. This is especially important with alcoholics whose social circle is liable to be composed of other alcoholics with similar attitudes.

Collusions are very important to detect and avoid since some people's attacks are exclusively the result of their contact with others whose Enemy agrees with and stimulates their own. The corner bar is a place where collusions are plentiful and always available; it is best to avoid it altogether. Very often, newly sober alcoholics want to socialize and drink sodas at their old hangout. I have never seen that work for long. The alcoholic either gets sucked in or eventually avoids bars altogether.

In one example of a collusion a man, after months of working on attacks that seemed to come on just before the group meeting on Mondays, realized that he had a standing telephone date with his parents on Sunday evenings. He hated the calls but was locked into them. He felt he could not get out of them. His parents always talked to him in veiled critical tones by asking questions about his work and his relationships. These questions came from their Enemy and stimulated an Enemy attack in him. ("You'll never amount to anything." "You'll never be loved.") When he realized that and decided not to call them for a month, he became free of attacks.

Eventually he reopened communication with them, but this time with an understanding of what he was and wasn't willing to accept in his conversations with them. In fact, he was able to educate them about the Enemy; and they stopped "laying their Enemy on him" and presumably on each other and themselves as well.

Collusions can come from anyone but tend to come from people who would like to control us and are angry at us because they can't—such as certain kinds of parents, spouses, or lovers, employers, teachers, preachers, and politicians. Drinkers are often annoyed at people who have quit and are liable to use all sorts of subtle and sometimes crude maneuvers to get them off the wagon.

This stage of the work is an intense period of analysis of the Enemy's tactics and techniques and the counter-tactics and -techniques which neutralize it. After some of this work, we hit on the effective method that seems to suddenly destroy the Enemy. It must be used every time the Enemy rears its ugly head—and it will. The person needs to practice, to be alert to renewed attacks, which, incidentally, will become more subtle as the Enemy tries to find new avenues around effective defenses. When an effective strategy is found, the point in the struggle is clearly marked by a sudden release from the great anxieties caused by intense attacks, so that the person is now in a whole new phase of well-being and feelings of O.K.ness, even though the attacks may continue at a much lower level of intensity and with less frequency.

These feelings of well-being arise from having developed techniques against Enemy attacks which demonstrate that it is wrong, that it is not really part of us, and that we can stop it from dominating our lives.

Sometimes someone will come to the group after a week of unsuccessful struggle and despondently describe his powerlessness in confronting the Enemy. Nothing seems to work; the Enemy has dominated his life for days. What to do?

It is important to become very specific about the time, place, and details of the attacks, and the strategies used to fight it. When did it happen? Where did it happen? What was the beginning of it? How did it proceed? And, especially, what was done to stop the Enemy? In doing this one finds what techniques are unsuccessful. The techniques need to be analyzed in order to understand the reason for their lack of success.

Other techniques need to be developed to replace those that didn't work. If turning a deaf ear didn't work, perhaps calling someone up and getting nurturing strokes will. If that doesn't work, maybe physical strokes are needed, and one needs to get a massage or run around the block. If massage or running don't work, maybe staging a shouting match with the Enemy will work. If a shouting match doesn't work, then perhaps one can develop finely tuned arguments to defeat the Enemy. If having a list of strokes written by the group doesn't work, perhaps it didn't because the list was kept under the pillow instead of hanging next to the bed where it can easily be seen. If arguing against the Enemy didn't work, perhaps it was done in a pleading rather than angry tone of voice. Eventually a technique that works will be found if the person, the therapist, and the group keep at it. The Enemy's hold will be weakened.

Fighting the Enemy is at the core of healing alcoholism. Of course, there are other important taks to be accomplished. Developing a competent problem-solving Adult, helping the Child rediscover joy and pleasure, developing satisfying stroke sources, finding a support subculture free of drug use in which loving confrontation is the rule and improving food and health habits are important, too.

17

We Are
What We Eat

I have always claimed that professional training in clinical psychology, psychiatry, social work, or any of the other "helping" professions is almost totally lacking in practical information which is helpful in working with people who have alcohol or other drug-abuse problems. Theories abound, but the really useful approaches are sadly lacking—especially when compared with Alcoholics Anonymous or other self-help groups.

One of the most amazing lacks of knowledge in the professional community of "alcohologists" concerns the importance of nutritional issues and ingestive habits for the alcoholic or, for that matter any person who shows signs of emotional disturbance. In my own professional training as a clinical psychologist, there was never any suggestion that mental state could be affected by what was eaten in the recent or distant past. Of course we knew that alcohol and other drugs were intoxicating substances, but that is where the information ended. No further connection was made between various foods and substances and people's states of mind.

Only after working for years among alcohol and drug-abuse "experts," many of whom were physicians, I realized for the first time that it was important to find out what so-called "psychotics" had been putting in their mouths recently. Believe it or not, it took working with people who had been using huge quantities of amphetamines to bring me this awareness. I had been trained to believe that the mind and the body are separate and that while what we eat can make us physically ill, the mind is somehow exempt from what we do to our bodies.

This mind-body separation which is a very strong belief in our culture is also the source of a lot of trouble for us. We really have come to believe the myth that there are two separate parts of us and that they can operate independently—especially that the mind is able to transcend the bodily plane, and disregard bodily matters.

True, a few people (and they are *very* few) are able to achieve a mental state in which their mind operates independently of the sensations of pain, hunger, or emotion, but these people achieve that state through intense bodily discipline—not by disregarding or neglecting their bodies. Yoga's intense long-term practice is aimed at learning how to relax in order to make meditation and detachment from the physical plane possible. Thus mind and body are united and our bodily states—all our bodily states—definitely affect our minds.

For me, who had a strong mind-body-split view as a psychologist, it was a surprise to realize that large doses of amphetamines can actually create a state of mind that looks every bit like those psychoses which I had learned were caused by internal mental conflicts. When I began to inquire closely into people's eating and sleeping habits prior to and during their emotional crises, I found that alcoholics tend to drink and stop eating. They often smoke excessively, drink a lot of coffee, and eat snacks and junk food almost exclusively. Their sleep patterns are often disturbed. I also began to realize that when a person drinks and manages to eat and sleep properly and is not especially addicted to cigarettes and coffee, the devastating health catastrophes that are so common to other alcoholics were often avoided; the drinking did not become as intense, and the recovery did not take as long.

Something that should have been obvious to me and my co-workers and which should have been taught to me in my training suddenly began to become clear to me: much of the distress that alcoholics suffer has to do with what they consume *other than alcohol.* An alcoholic's binge may have more to do with what he is putting in his mouth—*in addition to alcohol*—than with any other thing whether allergy, incurable disease, heredity, or script.

The most destructive drinking pattern that I've ever seen—one that is common with skid-row alcoholics—is the combination of cheap wine with little or no other food than the cheapest food available at the corner store: white bread, canned beans, jam or peanut butter, together with coffee, all of it laced with plenty of sugar and cigarettes.

Sugar (cheap wine is loaded with it) suppresses appetite, and so do cigarettes and coffee. Alcohol makes you sleepy at first, but a few hours later, it interferes with sleep. So does coffee, and for some people cigarettes cause sleeplessness, too.

The hardest time for an alcoholic is usually the evening. Characteristically, an alcoholic will start drinking after work. This will suppress his appetite. He will not eat a reasonable meal, especially if meals are not cooked for him and he has already lost his family milieu where regular meals are a routine. Instead he will eat a hot dog or a hamburger, a sweet roll, and a cup of coffee with lots of sugar. Most of this has no food value—only carbohydrates and fats. While he is drinking, he is smoking cigarettes. Sleeplessness and insomnia will be the natural outcome of this combination. The later at night it gets the more isolated and alone he will feel, the more fearful of his condition he becomes. Eventually he falls asleep at two or three o'clock in the morning after having overdosed with alcohol. He may wake up very early—way before anyone else does—shaky and sick, drink a cup of coffee, smoke some cigarettes, eat some junk food, and the drinking will start again.

This pattern is very typical of skid-row alcoholics, but it is also happening next door and down the street in Middletown, U.S.A. It may not be shockingly obvious, but all the elements are there: coffee, cigarettes, poor diet (including too much sugar and fats), sleeplessness, and usually, in addition, sleeping pills or other powerful tranquilizing medication. The effect can be just as devastating as living on skid row. The physical effects of this kind of a diet combined with the sleeplessness that goes with it should be obvious to anyone who thinks about it. Yet people who work with alcoholics don't ordinarily pay much attention to eating habits. It seems extremely important, and I can't imagine being effective in helping alcoholics without dealing with these problems in some way or another.

Even an interest in nutritional abuses as described above is not really sufficient. The problem is actually more serious and subtle than that. Recently Mr. Q. came to me because he was concerned about his drinking. He had a full-time job and a family, and he had been drinking socially for years; but he had noticed that alcohol was becoming more and more important in his daily life. He was concerned and wanted to do something about it. I asked him a few routine questions about his diet.

C.S.: How do you eat? Do you have a reasonably good diet?

Mr. Q.: Yes, I eat quite well. In fact, I eat too much.

C.S.: Well, tell me what you had to eat yesterday, for instance.

Mr. Q.: Okay, I had breakfast, lunch and dinner, like I do almost every day.

This would seem to be a clear enough answer, but I persisted.

C.S.: Let's be more specific. What did you have for breakfast?

Mr. Q.: I had some toast and cereal.

C.S.: Is that all?

Mr. Q.: Yes—what else? What do you mean?

C.S.: Well, did you have coffee? What did you have on your toast?

Mr. Q.: Oh, yes, I always have coffee. I have one cup of coffee first thing in the morning.

C.S.: Sugar?

Mr. Q.: Yes. Three teaspoons.

C.S.: Heaping?

Mr. Q.: Yes.

C.S.: Cigarettes?

Mr. Q.: Yes, a cigarette as soon as I get up.

C.S.: How many cigarettes by the time you take off for work?

Mr. Q.: I'm trying to cut down to one, but I usually have three. Lately, I've been having more. They get me going.

C.S.: Okay. What kind of bread?

Mr. Q.: Just regular white bread.

C.S.: Jam? Butter? What do you put on it?

Mr. Q.: I put margarine on it and I love jam, so I really pile it on.

C.S.: How many pieces of toast?

Mr. Q.: About three slices.

C.S.: Sugar in your cereal?

Mr. Q.: No, I like the sugar-frosted kind.

C.S.: Fruit?

Mr. Q.: Yes, canned fruit cocktail.

C.S.: So what did you eat next?

Mr. Q.: Lunch, I guess.

C.S.: Any snacks at the office?

Mr. Q.: Well, I usually have another cup of coffee and—

C.S.: With sugar, of course?

Mr. Q.: Yes, and I'll go to the vending machine around ten-thirty in the morning and buy a donut.

C.S.: Okay, let's talk about lunch. What did you have for lunch?

Mr. Q.: I'm trying to stay on a diet, so I had a salad.

C.S.: Dressing?

Mr. Q.: Yes, Thousand Island.

C.S.: Is that all?

Mr. Q.: Yes, except for some crackers. I also ate somebody else's crackers, and had more coffee.

C.S.: By now you must be really hungry.

Mr. Q.: Yes, I'm usually starved at lunch, but I try to keep what I eat down because of my diet and also because I don't want to spend a lot of money.

C.S.: Okay, what comes next?

Mr. Q.: Another cup of coffee in the afternoon. This is around three-thirty, and at this time I feel very sleepy and tired and am usually dying to have a drink. This is why I am beginning to worry about my drinking. I have been thinking about drinking a lot just before work ends, and I can hardly wait to get out. I used to go home and have my first drink, but my wife has been nagging me about it, so I stop at a bar and I have a martini.

C.S.: Anything with it?

Mr. Q.: Well, they usually have some snacks during Happy Hour—some deep-fried stuff or cheese—and I usually eat some of them.

C.S.: How many?

Mr. Q.: As many as I can get.

C.S.: Okay. What did you have for dinner?

Mr. Q.: Pretty good—my wife cooks balanced meals. Often I really don't like what she cooks—it's mostly for the kids—but last night she had frankfurters, mashed potatoes, and salad.

C.S.: Mashed potatoes out of a box, or actually potatoes that are mashed?

Mr. Q.: Oh, I don't know. I think they come from a box. They're instant potatoes.

C.S.: Anything on your potatoes? Sour cream?

Mr. Q.: We can't afford sour cream. I put a lot of margarine on them.

C.S.: How many frankfurters?

Mr. Q.: Three.

C.S.: What dressing on your salad?

Mr. Q.: Thousand Island. I know, you want to know if it was out of a bottle. Yes, out of a bottle.

C.S.: You're beginning to see the point of all these questions. Okay, any more the rest of the evening?

Mr. Q.: No more food, but a lot of wine.

C.S.: Are you sure? No snacks?

Mr. Q.: Let me see. I usually eat something around ten o'clock. Yes, I had some more toast and margarine and jam.

C.S.: How much did you drink?

Mr. Q.: I think I drank a bottle of wine before I got to bed. I used to drink two glasses, but now I'm up to a bottle or more, and that's worrying me.

I don't know how this description of Mr. Q.'s diet strikes you, but it strikes me as being a nightmare of malnutrition. If we total what he ate, it's about seven slices of white bread, one stick of margarine (four ounces), a cup and a half of sugar, half a head of lettuce, a handful of peas, four frankfurters, salad dressing, several deep-fried snacks and a generous assortment of the more than thousand different chemicals that are routinely added to our food.

No wonder Mr. Q. is hungry all the time. He thinks he eats too much. In fact, he's starving himself. No wonder he craves a drink before work is over. Alcohol is a very quick, accessible source of carbohydrates that satisfy his hunger cravings. No wonder he can't sleep. No wonder, in fact, his drinking is gone out of control. Look at him. He is overweight, saggy, tired, and devastated. One would assume that this has to do mostly with his drinking. In fact, it has to do with his overall diet—including his drinking. The coffee doesn't help; the cigarettes don't help either.

In fact, when Mr. Q. cleaned up his diet, his drinking went back to the previous more acceptable levels. However, educating Mr. Q. to the realities of food and diet was not easy. He was addicted to sugar, coffee, and cigarettes—a powerful addiction. It took months for him to bring his sugar consumption down, his processed carbohydrates down, his coffee down, his cigarettes and alcohol down. To have tried to ignore what he ate and to have worked only with his alcohol consumption would have been a completely different approach, and, I believe, dangerously ineffective. True, we immediately agreed for him to stop drinking altogether, and he did; but his craving for alcohol continued for months and coincidentally decreased when he straightened out his diet.

Alcoholics will complain of several symptoms their drinking makes better and will often blame their drinking on sleeplessness, nervousness, being cold, and not being able to warm up, hunger pangs and, of course, extreme cravings for alcohol. All of these symptoms can be caused by the alcoholic's diet, and all of them can be dealt with and reduced so that the desire for alcohol will be reduced as well.

Sleep Problems

Sleep problems are the major reason that people drink late at night, and night drinking is the royal road to alcoholism. In order to understand insomnia, we have to look at the whole day preceding it.

Naturally, drinking coffee will have an effect—especially within four or five hours of bedtime. People who suffer from insomnia should stop drinking coffee—or at least cut down drastically. Of course, quitting will probably cause drowsiness after lunch because people usually eat some kind of sugar at lunch, and sugar causes drowsiness after delivering a quick shot of energy. The usual antidote to that drowsiness is more coffee. So, sugar needs to be cut back too. The best solution is to eat a light lunch which is high in available protein and low in sugar. For a substitute to the usual mid-afternoon coffee and cigarette fix, one New Age nutritionist recommends a capsule of cayenne, or a glass of lemon juice with brewer's yeast together with a good stretch or a run around the block.

In the evening, insomniacs should not have coffee with dinner or after and should not smoke cigarettes for one hour before bedtime. Having eaten a nutritional well-balanced meal, and having some warm milk or herb tea (no black tea, which contains caffeine), just before going to bed will bring sleep in most situations, especially if there has been some physical exercise during the day.

Of course, people can keep themselves awake with worries—especially worries of not being able to sleep—and in those situations it is important that they be able to read in bed or watch television, or write or knit—some activity that can be easily put aside once they become drowsy. It is very useful to have a good reading light that will not disturb one's sleeping partner and which can be turned on in the middle of the night. It is especially important for people who have problems sleeping not to lie awake in the dark because that situation is one in which the Enemy tends to have an easy hold of the mind. Instead, they should turn on a light and pick up some light reading so that they can be awake for a while and then go back to sleep, instead of becoming agitated and panicked about losing sleep. Sleeping medication should be avoided as much as possible, but it can sometimes be effectively used to break a string of sleepless nights and ease the anxiety and tension of insomnia.

Cravings

Cravings for food, cigarettes, and alcohol are all related to each other. Very often people are undernourished even though they may be eating large quantities of food. This will cause them to be constantly hungry and to smoke cigarettes and drink coffee, since they do not want to eat. Cravings for alcohol can have a similar source. People's diet in this country is too heavy in white flour, refined sugar, and fats, all of which have essentially no food value. Making sure that a person is eating whole wheat flour products, that she is consuming enough fresh foods (vegetables that have recently been cut) and some form of easily digested low-fat protein, such as farmer's cheese or tofu, can do a great deal to decrease an alcoholic's craving for food, sugar, caffeine, and nicotine. People who must economize should know that it is possible to obtain excellent nutritional food in little-known ways and at low cost. Brown rice combined with beans is a rich source of protein although brown rice or beans alone are mostly a source of starch. It is possible to sprout alfalfa and sunflower seeds, lentils, and beans for a source of chemical-free greens rich in minerals, vitamins, and other nutrients.

Most important, people must realize that all packaged or processed foods are adulterated and nutritionally damaged and should be avoided. At the very least, people should read the ingredients list that appears on all packages with the understanding that the contents are listed in order of quantity, with the highest amount first.

Accordingly, it is good to look for the inevitable sugar, also listed as sucrose and dextrose, and note how high on the list it appears. The higher up, the more sugar the package contains. If it appears first, second, or third, the package should be avoided at all costs.

It is not the intention of this book to provide a complete nutritional guide, but just to point out that these are important issues and that they are not effectively taken care of by what is considered a "balanced" diet by trained dieticians, such as those who prepare foods for hospitals, institutions, and cafeterias. The art and science of nutrition has been neglected by the medical establishment and other professions that should know better. Recent modern knowledge about nutrition has yet to reach the general population. Instead we eat what we are told by the media and the processed-food industry, all of which—*without exception*—is nutritionally substandard. For a more comprehensive, generally available, coverage on the subject of nutrition, the best book to read, at the moment, is David Reuben's *Everything You Always Wanted to Know About Nutrition.*[1] As the infant science of modern nutrition develops more good books on the subject should become available and easily accessible.

Irritability and Nervousness

Unhappiness and nervousness, are usually attributed to psychological causes. As I explained before, I see all negative thoughts and energies as originating in the Enemy, which definitely resides in the mind sector of the person. But it is also important to recognize that irritability and nervousness can have chemical origins. Excessive smog, smoking, coffee, sugar, salt, and certain additives in most processed foods are all a potential source of nervousness and irritability. Any unpleasant bodily feelings are a springboard for the Enemy. Food additives like caffeine, food colors, MSG, calcium propionate, sulfur dioxide and other sulfites, benzoic acid, BHA/BHT, are known irritants in large amounts. No one knows what happens when these chemicals are combined with caffeine, nicotine and all the other noxious chemicals that go into our bodies. When a person is experienceing strong feelings of nervousness and irritability, let us not blindly assume that the source of those feelings is strictly psychological, but try to minimize all other possible sources to enhance his chance to go through a period of withdrawal from alcohol with a minimum of difficulty.

Unfortunately, because of the irritability that comes with stopping alcohol use, the reaction of someone who stops drinking is often an increased use of all the other harmful chemicals that he is using already. The person who stops drinking will usually drink more coffee, smoke more, and eat more. Snacks notoriously contain all sorts of poisonous chemicals, and it is therefore important for the alcoholic to recognize that alcohol is not the only harmful substance that he is consuming. He must remain conscious of all the other things he puts into his mouth and into his system while he is trying to stop drinking. Because snacks are important as pacifiers, it is a good idea to have good nutritious snacks available. Good snacks are carrot and celery sticks, sunflower seeds, peanuts in the shell, and a favorite of mine, popcorn sprinkled with nutritional yeast. In all of these, it is important to keep salt content low since salt itself can cause irritability.

Feelings of Coldness

Another physical reason that people give for their drinking is being chilly and cold. Alcohol is known to give a temporary feeling of warmth. Less known is the fact that it causes heat loss and eventually more chill. People often drink because they feel cold and have found drinking an effective way of temporarily warming up.

Here it is important to understand the several factors which could cause the kind of chill that would require one to have a drink. Cigarettes and coffee, which are both stimulants, constrict the blood vessels in the skin and cause feelings of coldness.

Drinking is often associated with lack of strokes and literal cravings for human warmth and being touched. Being cold at night, in bed, is another common occurrence, whose importance is often neglected. It is helpful to teach people how to dress warmly, and how to sleep warmly: to wear a nightshirt, to make sure to have enough warm blankets—preferably down, rather than electric, which tend to be irritating as well. It is useful to explain how hot beverages other than coffee and black tea can produce a feeling of warmth and how niacin, which is often lacking in the alcoholic diet, can do the same. It is useful as well, for a person who drinks to learn how to treat the skin to massages, warm comfortable organic clothing that contains cotton or wool, rather than synthetics, and pleasant comforting bedclothes.

And of course, kicking the smoking habit is a very important and life-giving change to make. Cigarette addiction is a whole subject in its own right. When they are ready to quit, people can get lots of information and help from *Kicking It* a book on how to stop smoking by David Geisinger.[2]

Some of the changes that are suggested in this chapter require a large modification in life-style. Nevertheless, even if they cannot be followed completely, or all at once, it is useful to be aware of the importance of some of the things mentioned here. This way, people can be conscious of how they may be adding to their difficulties through diet and other factors which are usually not associated with alcoholism. Alcoholics who are trying to stop drinking are fortunate if they have loved ones who are concerned enough to help them with these everyday details. If friends and family are not around, it is usually even more difficult to do what must be done. Nevertheless, it is important to keep all these factors in mind.

18

Favorite Hang-ups

It is not my intention here to fully discuss how to do therapy. That information is available in *Scripts People Live* [1] and in *Solving Women's Problems*. [2]

In this book, I address myself only to those ideas and methods that I have found specifically useful in dealing with alcoholics. In saying this, however, I want to make clear that outside of the fact that alcoholics drink too much, I have not found them to be particularly different from other people. Once an alcoholic stops drinking and has been sober for a few weeks, they are indistinguishable from other people who may need therapy. They are neither more passive, nor more aggressive, nor more passive-aggressive, nor in possession of more personality or thinking disorders than the run-of-the-mill citizen. This assertion is corroborated by Armor who, in *Alcoholism and Treatment*, [3] agrees that "a large number of studies have generally failed to identify and specify personality traits that clearly differentiate alcoholics from other deviant groups or from persons judged to be normal." Often, in fact, ceasing the drinking, an alcoholic feels extremely well and is a well-adjusted individual who seemingly does not even need psychotherapy.

In this chapter, I will focus on some of the patterns or hang-ups which tend to appear in the lives of alcoholics. This is not to say that these same factors are not apparent in the lives of other clients, or in the lives of all people; but just to say that they are often found in alcoholics and are therefore worth our consideration.

Don't Think, Drink

One of the patterns which I have observed with alcoholics and other people who abuse intoxicating substances is that very often, under circumstances of stress, when a problem presents itself, there's a tendency to use the drug to escape the strain. Some people learn that under difficult circumstances, the most effective thing to do is to literally sit down, clear their minds, and think about the problem and its possible solutions. This problem-solving attitude includes seeking out other people who are respected for their capacity to think and solve problems and together to map out a strategy to deal with the situation.

Alcoholics and other drug abusers very often deal with problems by drinking instead of thinking. Commonly people who abuse drugs are under the definite impression that the drug helps them think and solve problems. They have observed that when the mind does not function well under conditions of anxiety, their drug of choice acts as a mental lubricant, so that where it was once impossible to think clearly and every thought was painful and difficult, the mental machinery now pumps along like a well-tuned engine. But while the subjective experience of easy and brilliant thinking is real enough, it does not necessarily reflect very effective, objective problem-solving. In fact, the type of thinking that occurs under drugs is often riddled with fantasy and wish fulfillment and does not reflect the workings of reality very well at all. Even if good ideas are occasionally generated in this frame of mind, they are ordinarily lost in the fog of intoxication. Consequently, when people drink instead of thinking, nothing is accomplished. The pain that is postponed has to be faced all over again in the future.

The ego state that is capable of thinking in a direct and concentrated way is the Adult. The Adult can be exercised like muscles are exercised and it is important for an alcoholic or any other drug abuser to consciously decide to think instead of drinking. Very often, in group-therapy sessions, I have had the experience of asking the people who use drugs how they feel, or why they did a certain thing and their answer, very often, comes back: "I don't know."

My retort when somebody says "I don't know," is "Well, think about it, figure it out, concentrate."

Sandy reports that she had a huge fight with her husband which started when he came home the other night and dinner was not ready. She felt rather guilty about not having cooked his dinner and eventually got drunk after the fight.

C.S.: Why didn't you have dinner ready when your husband came home?

Sandy: I don't know. I just didn't.

C.S.: Well, think about it. What was going on?

Sandy: I told you, I don't know. I just didn't.

C.S.: Sandy, I want you to think about it. There must have been a reason, and maybe it was even a good reason, so let's try to find out. Why don't you relax and concentrate and try to put yourself back at the time and tell us why you didn't cook that dinner.

Sandy: Well, I was angry, and I didn't feel like cooking—that's all.

C.S.: What were you angry at?

Sandy: I don't know.

C.S.: Think about it.

Sandy: Well, I was angry at Jack because I had been asking him for weeks to have dinner out, and he kept promising that he would as soon as possible. But he never remembers, and we just don't ever go out.

C.S.: Okay, so you were angry at Jack. How did that cause you not to cook dinner?

Sandy: That's obvious. What a ridiculous question.

C.S.: Well, I'm not so sure it's obvious. Anyway, let's make it real clear. What brought you from being angry at Jack to not cooking dinner?

Sandy: I was angry at him and I realized that when he comes home he expects to be fed like a king and I wanted to annoy him and so I figured that if I didn't cook dinner he would be plenty annoyed.

C.S.: Did you also think that if dinner wasn't ready he might also take you out for dinner just because there wasn't any dinner at home?

Sandy: Yes. Isn't that ridiculous? Instead of that, he started screaming at me, and we didn't go out, and we didn't eat, and instead of that, I got drunk.

This is a simple example showing that although Sandy was originally unable to explain her behavior, once she thought about it, it became logical and understandable. From her understanding of why she did not cook dinner for Jack and how that was based on her anger, she also was able to develop a strategy to deal with the problem. She decided that she had to do something about her cooking all the time and to ask Jack to participate in the house chores. She did, and eventually she took a part-time job so that Jack did not have to work so hard. They both became more involved in the duties and obligations of cooking, and they also went out to eat more often.

Sandy tends to assume that she cannot understand and think through what's going on. Therefore she deals with her confusion by drinking. Yet, if she simply concentrates, she can actually understand and solve some of the difficult situations that she encounters in her daily life. "Think, don't drink" is a relevant motto in this situation.

I'd Rather Not Talk About It

Another pattern in alcoholics and other people who harm themselves to the point of being ashamed of themselves or who find themselves powerless in a way that causes them embarrassment and humiliation, is the overwhelming tendency to avoid discussing the embarrassing realities of their everyday lives. Things are discussed on a sort of semitheoretical level that never really touches the actual facts of the situation.

For instance, Peter, an alcoholic, seemed to be quite willing to discuss his private life, to talk about sex, about his drinking bouts, and so on. At first blush, he seemed very unashamed and candid. But it was a characteristic experience when listening to him that one never really understood just exactly what was happening. If there was drinking, one didn't really know much about it. How much did he drink? Did he throw up? Did he fall down? How long did he drink? What were the details of his latest binge?

Peter found it extremely difficult to go into details. If pressed, he would blush and become angry and turn on the questioner,

saying, "Why are you bugging me? Why do you want to get into
the gory details? This is nobody's business but my own. I'd rather
not talk about it." He was extremely embarrassed about these
events and found it very painful to discuss them, so he circum-
vented them while giving the *impression* of discussing them. In not
talking about the details of his everyday life, he created a mistaken
impression and also kept himself aloof from other people who
tended not to take a serious and deep concern in his situation. With
Peter, it turned out to be extremely important to press him for the
details, the specific transactions, the actual happenings of his everyday life.

Once Peter was complaining that he recently felt bored in his
relationship with his wife, and that this boredom caused him to
think about drinking almost all the time.

"Things aren't the way they used to be; it's a routine that we
just can't get out of. We just don't have any fun."

At this point, the members of the group started making suggestions along recreational lines, such as "Why don't you go to a play
(or on a trip) (or play Scrabble)?" But I got the impression that
Peter had not really stated what his boredom was all about. I
couldn't get a real feeling of what he was talking about, so I
questioned him further.

"I don't really understand what you're talking about. What is it
that is different from the way it used to be? You don't go out so
much? You don't go dancing? You don't take drives to the country?"

"It has nothing to do with that. It's just that she and I together
don't have any fun."

"How do you mean that?"

"Well, you know. In our relations."

The word "relations" set off a bell in my head: "You mean in
your sexual relations?"

"Yeah, what else?"

"Oh, I didn't realize that that was what you were talking about.
Well, what is it like? Are you not having sex as often as you used to,
or is it just not as much fun? What is it?"

"Now you're getting personal."

"Of course I'm getting personal. How else are we going to

figure out what you're talking about? Are you willing to explain it?"

"Well, I'd rather not talk about it; I don't talk about my sex life with people."

"I think you're going to have to do it. Otherwise we won't have any idea of what you're saying and we'll just beat around the bush, so to speak. What do you think?"

"Okay, sex is boring. It doesn't feel good like it used to."

"How do you mean that?"

(Blushing) "Well, I'm having trouble . . . you know, getting off . . ."

"So that's what you were talking about. No wonder you're upset. You know, it's very interesting how unclear this was to begin with. Can you see how everyone thought that you were talking about something completely different? We need to get into your sex life if we're going to talk about this at all."

"Well, I don't feel I can do that at all. I feel it's really nobody's business."

"Why not? Are you embarrassed?"

"Sure!"

"Well, I think it's important that you overcome . . . (haha) this embarrassment and that you learn to be willing to speak about these things with other people. I bet that's one of the reasons why in the past you have gone back to drinking. You aren't able to openly discuss your situation with other people. You tend to speak indirectly. There are probably a lot of Enemy messages in your head which need to be exposed. If you keep them inside and don't discuss them, they will be very hard to stop. What do you think? Would you be willing to do this?"

"I guess it's probably a good idea. Okay."

This is an example of the kind of resistance to frank discussion of the ups and downs of everyday life that alcoholics often exhibit. An excellent solution is a group in which everything is dealt with frankly by everyone. The cooperative contract with its "No Secrets" clause is very helpful in this respect. In fact, whether or not the cooperative contract is used, a group in which the avoidance of certain embarrassing subjects is allowed can't possibly be fully effective. When complete, frank discussion becomes the rule in a group, each person who joins learns to overcome his reluctance as he sees others speak frankly. This process is very difficult for some whose Enemy is dead set to make them ashamed of their personal lives. The messages, often taught by parents ("Don't talk about it." "It's nobody's business but your own." "They'll laugh at you.") can be extremely strong, and it is important to give people time and space to overcome them, while at the same time not accepting them.

Can't Feel a Thing Unless I'm High

Another area in which alcholics need help is in the expression of feelings. The drug abuser's open expression of feelings usually does not occur when she is sober. While sober, the alcoholic usually feels guilty. Her behavior tends to be circumspect and uptight as she tries to keep her emotions under control. This leads to a vicious circle in which, after a while, those emotions get bottled up and seek expression which, the alcoholic knows full well, comes easily by taking the cork out of the bottle. This eventually leads to drinking.

When intoxicated or high, people's feelings flow easily. There is an experience of pleasure and release which becomes associated with the use of the drug; just thinking about it can bring on the first stages of relaxation. During the alcoholic episode, a person will rage, cry, laugh, rant and rave, only to wake up next day to confront the havoc that this unbridled expression of emotions has created. This is followed by another period of emotional constriction which creates a new buildup of emotions that with their pressure creates the next act of the melodrama. Instead of profiting from the free flow of emotion, people suffer guilt and persecution.

In order to facilitate the guilt-free flow of emotions during a sober period, the use of body-work sessions has been found to be extremely effective. Body work, a method of therapy first used by Wilhelm Reich, is essentially an opportunity for people to contact, in an atmosphere of safety and encouragement, those feelings that usually seek expression through drug abuse. These sessions are designed specifically as an occasion for emotional release as opposed to the group sessions, which are primarily discussions and problem-solving meetings in which the Adult ego state has a primary role. Body-work sessions are a place in which the innermost feelings and experiences of the person are encouraged to come to the surface.

I do about one body-work session a month, which is open to all of the people in all of my groups. Usually between eight and twelve people attend. The body-work session lasts two or more hours. It takes place in a large room where people can lie down on the floor and have enough space to move around. We start with a brief discussion of what each person wants to accomplish during the session, and make a body-work contract for the session. Typical contracts are "Getting angry," "Crying," "Feeling good," "Releasing tension," "Getting in touch with my feelings," "Relaxing," and so on.

I start by asking everyone to lie down comfortably. When people come to a body-work session, they know to dress comfortably and to bring a favorite blanket or comforter in case they get cold which is often the case in the beginning part of the session. After everyone is comfortable, I give some instructions:

> The purpose of body work is to provide an opportunity for people to speak from and with their bodies. In group therapy we speak the language of the Adult, with words, mostly. The culture sanctions only that which comes from the "rational" part of ourselves and we have no permission to express the language of the body.
>
> In this session it is O.K. to express what your body has to say. The kinds of things that people do when they express what we feel in our bodies would probably create difficulties in the outside world. We provide a situation here where there is total safety. You will not be hurt for anything you do. You need feel no embarrassment or fear. The worst that could happen is that somebody else doing this work does not like whatever you are doing, and they may say so. But then you don't have to stop as long as you're not physically injuring anyone, and I and the people assisting me will make sure that you don't accidentally hit or hurt someone or yourself.
>
> It doesn't matter what you do with your body, what

posture you assume, what movement you make, whether you cry or scream or yell; it's all O.K., and you won't get criticized. Remember the cooperative contract we have in our groups. One rule is that you'll keep no secrets. To keep back a feeling is actually keeping a secret, and so, really, you are expected to express whatever you feel. In addition, of course, keep in mind your own particular body-work contract for this session. But remember, first and foremost, that this is a situation where you are to fully express what you feel, without any shame or holding back. In other words, I am saying you should feel safe, protected and with permission to do whatever you want to do.

These statements are designed to create a sense of trust and safety so the person can effectively deal with the strong messages which we all hear from our Enemy whenever we are about to express a strong feeling. Typically the Enemy will say things like "You are making a fool of yourself" or "This is childish and immature. Stop it!" or "People will hate you for being so crude." My reassuring statements coming from my own Ally provide the participants with ammunition against these injunctions from the Enemy.

The knowledge that I and the people assisting me are all here to provide permission and protection for this work is essential to effective body-work. Having accomplished that purpose, I continue:

I want to explain to you that the whole business of becoming aware of bodily feelings is basically a retuning, a refocusing of your attention. The feelings are actually there all the time, but we tend not to pay attention. Subtle feelings such as slight irritation, sadness, embarrassment are squelched. We notice only strong feelings like anger, pain, cold, or fear. I'd like you to start by simply focusing in on whatever it is that you're conscious of right now; pay attention to whatever is occupying your consciousness. Consciousness is not limited by this room and this moment. Right now you might be in the past or in the future or in another galaxy. Pay attention to where you are right now and when you have a clear idea, speak out and say where you are so we all can hear. I'll give you some time to get in touch with that. You will probably be aware of things like aches and pains. Or you might be preoccupied with an argument you had yesterday, or an examination tomorrow. Don't try to change what is going on in your mind; it will surely change by itself as we proceed. Slowly your thoughts will lose some of their primacy and the contents of your consciousness will change, and you'll start feeling other things. As you lie there and relax and notice what happens, you will discover there is a subtle shift in your consciousness. The focus of your attention is probably shifting down from somewhere in your head to somewhere lower in your body; your chest, abdomen, legs. And your consciousness is going to be less pictures, images, and words, and more feelings. The change is subtle; it doesn't happen instantly. Sometimes it takes time to start this process, and it also takes time to terminate it. You will have all the time you need. For instance, if you're walking down the street and you suddenly get a fright, your whole body is involved and it may take a half an hour to get over the effects of that. We aren't capable of beginning or ending our emotions the way we can begin and end thoughts. Our mind is like a computer—it can be turned on and off—but our emotions are different, they don't start or stop growing on command.

If we pay close attention to our feelings, we will notice what we think are peculiar things, feelings of floating, hollowness, or heaviness and different strange sensations like tingling or tight bands around some part of the body or energy fields, streaming sensations or what-have-you. These sensations can be alarming. People who feel them can get scared that they are losing their minds, which is in fact true. You are being encouraged to lose your mind, but remember that it is perfectly safe. You can get it back anytime you want. You are not really losing it—just setting it aside for a while. If you get scared, however, say so and if you want something ask for it. We will be here for anything you need. If you need a pillow to hit, or an extra blanket because you feel cold, or someone to hold your hand or hug or massage you—or if you need a tissue or something to spit or throw up into, just ask. We are here to take care of your needs while you explore or abandon yourself to your feelings.

At this point it is not unusual for some people to begin to feel and express strong emotions. Someone might start crying or say that he is scared or worried. But most people don't enter the process as easily. Usually at this point people are feeling cold, puzzled, worried, uneasy. In order to facilitate their work, I speak to them about breathing:

How we breathe has a lot to do with how much we feel and also perhaps how we feel. Not breathing deeply has the effect of constricting your feelings, and breathing deeply has the effect of fanning your feelings like embers in a fire. If you blow into them, the embers will glow and sometimes flames will break out if the fuel conditions are right. It's the same with feelings; breathing will make them more vivid, and sometimes it will cut them loose into a roar.

I'm going to teach you a little bit about breathing and encourage you to breathe deeply in order to facilitate your contact with your bodily feelings.

At this point I give a brief exercise in thoracic and abdominal breathing, teaching the difference and then showing how to combine the two in order to maximize respiration. I make sure that people are inhaling and exhaling fully:

As you breathe more fully, you are going to inevitably have to make some noise. Don't control that noise. Don't hold it back. Let it flow. Remember what a dog that is breathing heavily, sounds like. It makes noise. Open up your throats. Make any noise that naturally, normally accompanies that kind of breathing for you. Breathe deeply and well, opening up your throat as much as you can, breathing deeply, through your mouth, both ways, in and out.

Now I'd like you to exaggerate the sounds. We are very limited with our sounds. I'd like you to emphasize, dramatize it, say any thoughts or words that come into your minds.

Don't worry about being foolish, say, express, anything you feel with sounds, whether they are words or grunts or laughter or sighs or screams.

This is how the session begins. After this point I just encourage whatever expressions naturally happen, attend to people's needs, but mostly let them run through whatever flow of emotion or feeling that comes. Usually about one-third of the people have a powerful and meaningful emotional release which often leaves them with a feeling of rebirth or a born-again experience. The rest go through a variety of lesser but mostly satisfying experiences of crying, anger, well-being, or relaxation. A few find themselves completely shut down, cut off, alienated. Some even leave the session. I do not do anything to change this, except to encourage whatever people feel they want to do. I let the flow of emotions take its own course, encourage it here and there, and let the combined effect of all the factors in the situation create each person's individual experience.

People are strongly influenced by how safe they feel, by their own life situation of the moment, by who is assisting me, by what others in the room are doing and feeling, by their contracts, and I daresay by the weather and the phases of the moon.

The body-work session facilitates emotional storm and release. As it proceeds, it feels like just that: a storm at sea. Feelings will come in waves of deep sadness, wild anger, uncontrollable laughter which will affect all of us in some way or another. The combined experience is cleansing and tends to have a strongly remembered effect which will be the basis for discussion at the next group session. After a period which may vary between about forty-five minutes and an hour and a half, the storm subsides. Everyone becomes quiet. When that lull comes, I ask whoever is ready to sit up to do so, and when everyone feels complete and feels ready to sit up, each person spends some time sharing what she or he experienced. The meeting may end with a group hug or a circle in which all hold hands.

People will confront their emotional issues fully in a later session if not in the first one. Their tendencies to be afraid, or to Rescue, or to become bottled up and hopeless, their anger or sadness sooner or later come to the surface and become obvious.

Some will never experience an emotional release, but most will sooner or later. In any case, body work is an exceptionally valuable experience for alcoholics. Since I have begun offering it regularly, I have experienced greatly increased success in my work with this group.

Readers who perceive the power of this process will realize also that it is not available to most people in their everyday lives. It is hard to find a situation in which we can let go in safety and with full encouragement. Our society simply doesn't support that kind of behavior. Similar abandon can be found only in spectator sports, some very rare churches, or at wild parties which are usually stimulated by alcohol, or in one's car while driving on the freeway.

Nevertheless, the expression of feeling can be legitimized in the alcoholic (or in all of us, for that matter) in a number of different ways. Body work is only the most effective and dramatic. Let us realize that the true expression of feeling is our birthright, that not to claim that birthright makes our lives joyless and susceptible to alcohol and other drug abuse. The liberation of our feelings is a basic task in healing alcoholism.

19

Summary

Alcoholism is not a disease; therefore, the solutions to alcoholism are not medical. Drugs, hospitals, and physicians are not of any particular value in healing alcoholism.

Alcoholism is not incurable. It is an acquired condition different from person to person, based partly on innate biochemical sensitivity to alcohol, partly on social pressure to drink, and partly on the emotional, thinking, and nutritional habits of the alcoholic. Alcoholism can be healed, and a few former alcoholics are evidently able to return to normal drinking though the majority either can't or won't.

Alcoholics Anonymous is a valuable source of help in providing very effective, easily available, frequent and free meetings for all alcoholics in need of help. On the other hand, A.A. is also an overbearing organization with a powerful dogma which is preventing different, possibly valuable points of view from being expressed to the detriment of the advance of knowledge in the alcoholism field.

The physical factor responsible for alcoholism is the addictive properties of alcohol which for some people are extremely powerful combined with the poor dietary habits (cigarettes, coffee, sugar, adulterated food) which are usually associated with alcohol abuse.

The social factors responsible for alcoholism are the intense social pressures to drink coming from the alcoholic's family, social, and work circle, from the media, and from the fact that alcohol is almost universally associated with recreation.

The psychological factors responsible for alcoholism reside in the Enemy. The Enemy is a collection of harmful messages that have been adopted by the person and that interfere with thinking, feeling, getting strokes, and being aware of one's body. The Enemy continually attacks the person's O.K.-ness.

The specific combination of all the physical social and psychological factors are different for each alcoholic. Alcoholics are not significantly different from all other people. They simply represent the most extreme and visible sector of a population that is poisoning itself with a variety of chemicals, drugs, and environmental pollutants.

A major factor in alcoholism is the participation of alcoholics and their circle in the Alcoholic game with its three roles: Victim, Rescuer, and Persecutor. These roles must be avoided by anyone who wishes to help the alcoholic.

In order to avoid the role of Rescuer, a helper needs to make sure that a mutually agreed upon contract exists in the relationship with the alcoholic. Avoiding Rescuing is the best way to avoid subsequent, inevitable participation in the game as Persecutor or Victim. Staying aloof from the game roles is a prerequisite to helpful interaction with the alcoholic.

Once game-free, the helper works by providing loving confrontation, that is: relevant, objective information in a context of warmth and protection. Sobriety, frank discussion of life problems, learning how to solve problems and how to obtain strokes, changing dietary habits, emotional release, body work, developing an Ally, and Antabuse are some powerful aids in healing alcoholism.

Notes

PREFACE

1. Claude M. Steiner, *Games Alcoholics Play* (New York: Grove Press, 1971).
2. David J. Armor, J. Michael Polich and Harriet B. Stambul, *Alcoholism and Treatment* (New York: John Wiley & Sons, 1978), p. 99.
3. Claude M. Steiner, *Scripts People Live* (New York: Grove Press, 1974).

INTRODUCTION

1. *Alcoholics Anonymous* (New York: Alcoholics Anonymous Publishing Company, 1955).
2. American Medical Association, *Manual on Alcoholism* (Washington, D.C.: American Medical Association, 1967).
3. Thomas Lathrop Stedman, *Stedman's Medical Dictionary*, 20th ed. (Baltimore: Williams and Wilkins, 1962).
4. Thomas S. Szasz, *The Myth of Mental Illness* (New York: Hoeber-Harper, 1961).
5. American Medical Association, *Manual on Alcoholism.*
6. Jerome D. Frank, "The Role of Hope in Psychotherapy," *International Journal of Psychiatry* 5(1968): 383–95.

CHAPTER 1

1. Eric Berne, *Games People Play* (New York: Grove Press, 1964).

CHAPTER 2

1. David J. Armor, J. Michael Polich and Harriet B. Stambul, *Alcoholism and Treatment* (New York: John Wiley & Sons, 1978), p. 106.

2. James R. Milam, *The Emergent Comprehensive Concept of Alcoholism* (Kirkland, Washington: ACA Press, 1970).

CHAPTER 3

1. Eric Berne, *Games People Play* (New York: Grove Press, 1964).
2. Stephen B. Karpman, "Script Drama Analysis," *Transactional Analysis Bulletin* 7, 26 (1968): 39–43.

CHAPTER 7

1. Claude M. Steiner, *TA Made Simple* (Berkeley: Claude Steiner, 1971). This pamphlet may be ordered for $2.00 from TA Simple, Box 5155, Berkeley, CA 94705.
2. Eric Berne, *Transactional Analysis in Psychotherapy* (New York: Grove Press, 1961).
3. Eric Berne, *Beyond Games and Scripts* (New York: Grove Press, 1976).

CHAPTER 8

1. John R. Wikse, *About Possession: The Self as Private Property* (University Park, Pa.: Pennsylvania State University Press, 1977).
2. Wayne W. Dyer, *Pulling Your Own Strings* (New York: Funk & Wagnalls, 1978).
3. Michael Korda, *Success! How Every Man and Woman Can Achieve It* (New York: Random House, 1976).
4. Robert J. Ringer, *Looking Out for No. 1* (New York: Fawcett Books, 1978).

CHAPTER 10

1. Claude M. Steiner (ed.), *Readings in Radical Psychiatry* (New York: Grove Press, 1975).
2. Hogie Wyckoff, *Solving Women's Problems* (New York: Grove Press, 1977).
3. Steiner, *Readings in Radical Psychiatry*.
4. Bob Schwebel, "Trashing the Stroke Economy," *Issues in Radical Therapy* 18 (Spring 1977): 13–16. Available from Box 5039, Berkeley, CA 94705.

CHAPTER 13

1. Claude M. Steiner, *Scripts People Live* (New York: Grove Press, 1974).

CHAPTER 17

1. David Reuben, *Everything You Always Wanted to Know About Nutrition* (New York: Simon and Schuster, 1978).
2. David L. Geisinger, *Kicking It* (New York: Grove Press, 1979).

CHAPTER 18

1. Claude M. Steiner, *Scripts People Live* (New York: Grove Press, 1974).
2. Hogie Wyckoff, *Solving Women's Problems* (New York: Grove Press, 1977).
3. David J. Armor, J. Michael Polich and Harriet B. Stambul, *Alcoholism and Treatment* (New York: John Wiley & Sons, 1978).

Bibliography

Alcoholics Anonymous. *Alcoholics Anonymous*. New York: Alcoholics Anonymous Publishing Company, 1955.

American Medical Association. *Manual on Alcoholism*. Washington, D.C.: American Medical Association, 1967.

Armor, David J., Polich, J. Michael and Stambul, Harriet B. *Alcoholism and Treatment*. New York: John Wiley & Sons, 1978.

Berne, Eric. *Beyond Games and Scripts*. New York: Grove Press, 1976.

———. *Games People Play*. New York: Grove Press, 1964.

———. *Transactional Analysis in Psychotherapy*. New York: Grove Press, 1961.

Dyer, Wayne W. *Pulling Your Own Strings*. New York: Funk & Wagnalls, 1978.

Frank, Jerome D. "The Role of Hope in Psychotherapy." *International Journal of Psychiatry* 5 (1968): 383–95.

Geisinger, David L. *Kicking It*. New York: Grove Press, 1979.

Karpman, Stephen B. "Script Drama Analysis." *Transactional Analysis Bulletin* 7, 26 (1968):39–43.

Korda, Michael. *Success! How Every Man and Woman Can Achieve It*. New York: Random House, 1976.

Milam, James R. *The Emergent Comprehensive Concept of Alcoholism*. Kirkland, Washington: ACA Press, 1970.

Reuben, David. *Everything You Always Wanted to Know About Nutrition*. New York: Simon and Schuster, 1978.

Ringer, Robert J. *Looking Out for No. 1*. New York: Fawcett Books, 1978.

Schwebel, Bob. "Trashing the Stroke Economy." *Issues in Radical Therapy* 18 (Spring 1977):13–16.

Stedman, Thomas Lathrop. *Stedman's Medical Dictionary*. 20th ed. Baltimore: Williams and Wilkins, 1962.

Steiner, Claude M. *Games Alcoholics Play*. New York: Grove Press, 1971.

————. (ed.). *Readings in Radical Psychiatry*. New York: Grove Press, 1975.

————. *Scripts People Live*. New York: Grove Press, 1974.

————. *TA Made Simple*. Berkeley: Claude M. Steiner, 1971.

Szasz, Thomas S. *The Myth of Mental Illness*. New York: Hoeber-Harper, 1961.

Wikse, John R. *About Possession: The Self as Private Property*. University Park, Pa.: Pennsylvania State University Press, 1977.

Wyckoff, Hogie. *Solving Women's Problems*. New York: Grove Press, 1977.

Index